It's another great book from CGP...

If you can read this, you obviously know a fair bit about English Language.
But to do well at GCSE, you'll need to be able to analyse it in a lot more detail...

Not to worry. This brilliant CGP Revision Guide covers all the skills you'll need,
with notes, examples, exam-style texts, sample answers and more
— all perfectly matched to the Grade 9-1 WJEC Eduqas course.

We've also included fully worked exam papers with graded answers, plus top
advice for the exams! So now you've got no excuse not to mind your language.

CGP — still the best! ☺

Our sole aim here at CGP is to produce the highest quality books —
carefully written, immaculately presented and dangerously close to being funny.

Then we work our socks off to get them out to you
— at the cheapest possible prices.

CONTENTS

Section One — Exam Basics

Exam Structure..1
The Assessment Objectives 2
Planning Answers 3
P.E.E.D. 4
Using Examples 5
Writing Well 6
Reading with Insight 8
Spelling, Punctuation and Grammar 10

Section Two — Reading: Understanding Texts

Information and Ideas 12
Audience 14
Writer's Purpose 15
Informative Texts 16
Entertaining Texts 17
Texts that Argue or Persuade 18
Texts that Advise 19
Writer's Viewpoint and Attitude 20
Literature 21
Literary Non-Fiction 22
19th-Century Texts 23

Section Three — Reading: Language and Structure

Tone 25
Style and Register 26
Words and Phrases 27
Metaphors and Similes 29
Analogy 30
Personification 31
Alliteration and Onomatopoeia 32
Irony 33
Sarcasm 34
Rhetoric 35
Bias 36
Descriptive Language 37
Narrative Viewpoint 38
Structure — Non-Fiction Texts 39
Structure — Fiction Texts 40
Sentence Forms..42
Presentation 44

CONTENTS

Section Four — Writing: Creative and Non-Fiction

Writing with Purpose 46
Writing for an Audience 48
Creative Writing 50
Writing Articles 53
Writing Leaflets 56
Travel Writing 57
Writing Reports and Essays 58
Writing Reviews 59
Writing Speeches 60
Writing Letters 61

Section Five — Paper 1: Sample Exam and Graded Answers

Sample Exam — Paper 1 62
Literature Extract 64
Graded Answer — Question A1 65
Graded Answers — Question A2 66
Graded Answers — Question A3 68
Graded Answers — Question A4 70
Graded Answers — Question A5 72
Graded Answers — Section B 74

Section Six — Paper 2: Sample Exam and Graded Answers

Sample Exam — Paper 2 76
21st-Century Source 78
19th-Century Source 79
Graded Answers — Question A1 80
Graded Answers — Question A2 81
Graded Answers — Question A3 83
Graded Answers — Question A4 84
Graded Answers — Question A5 86
Graded Answers — Question A6 88
Graded Answers — Question B1 90
Graded Answers — Question B2 92

Glossary 94
Index 96

Published by CGP

Editors:
Joe Brazier
Emma Crighton
Holly Poynton
Louise Taylor

With thanks to Glenn Rogers and John Sanders for the proofreading.
With thanks to Ana Pungartnik for the copyright research.

Acknowledgements:

With thanks to iStockphoto.com for permission to use the images on pages 21, 28, 57, 70 & 80.

Letter on page 24 to Princess (later Queen) Victoria from King Leopold I of Belgium, August 1832, from The Letters of Queen Victoria, Volume 1 (of 3), 1837-1843.

With thanks to Atlantic Books for permission to use the extract from JMG Le Clézio 'Desert' on pages 64-65.

With thanks to Ross Parry / Yorkshire Post for permission to use the article on page 78.

Text on page 79 'The County Unit in Educational Organization' by Lawton B. Evans, from The Granite Monthly, A New Hampshire Magazine, Volume 11, 1896.

For copyright reasons, this book can only be sold in the UK and Commonwealth (excluding Canada).

Every effort has been made to locate copyright holders and obtain permission to reproduce sources.
For those sources where it has been difficult to trace the copyright holder of the work, we would be grateful
for information. If any copyright holder would like us to make an amendment to the acknowledgements,
please notify us and we will gladly update the book at the next reprint. Thank you.

ISBN: 978 1 78294 371 6
Printed by Elanders Ltd, Newcastle upon Tyne.
Clipart from Corel®

Based on the classic CGP style created by Richard Parsons.

Exam Structure

Understanding the structure of your exams can take some of the stress out of sitting them. If you know what you're up against, you'll have a huge head start, leaving you free to swan off into the sunset with all the marks...

You will sit two different exam papers

1) Your GCSE in English Language will be examined over <u>two</u> separate exam papers. <u>Paper 1</u> (or 'Component 1') focuses on <u>fiction</u>, and <u>paper 2</u> (or 'Component 2') focuses on <u>non-fiction</u>.

2) Both papers are split into <u>two</u> sections:

- <u>Section A</u> contains <u>reading</u> questions, which test your ability to <u>understand</u> and <u>analyse</u> texts.

- <u>Section B</u> tests your ability to <u>write</u> texts <u>of your own</u>.

Fig 1: Candidate preparing to swan off into the sunset.

Read the source texts carefully

For <u>paper 1</u>, there will be a question paper, <u>one</u> extract from a work of literary fiction from the <u>20th century</u> and a separate answer book. You will have <u>1 hour 45 minutes</u> to complete this paper.

> Section A (reading) will usually be made up of <u>5 questions</u> that are worth a total of <u>40 marks</u>.
>
> - You should spend about <u>10 minutes</u> reading through the text and the questions, then about <u>50 minutes</u> writing your answers.
>
>   *See p.2 for more about the assessment objectives.*
>
> - You'll be tested on <u>assessment objectives 1, 2 and 4</u> in this section.
>
> Section B (writing) is worth <u>40 marks</u>. There'll be a <u>choice</u> of tasks, but you only need to do <u>one</u>.
>
> - For this task, you should spend about <u>10 minutes</u> planning and <u>35 minutes</u> writing.
>
> - You'll be tested on <u>assessment objectives 5 and 6</u> in this section.

PAPER 1

For <u>paper 2</u>, there will be a question paper, <u>two</u> non-fiction sources — one from the <u>19th century</u> and one from the <u>21st century</u> — and a separate answer book. You will have <u>2 hours</u> to complete this paper.

> Section A (reading) will usually have <u>6 questions</u> that are worth a total of <u>40 marks</u>.
>
> - You should spend about <u>10 minutes</u> reading through the texts and the questions, then about <u>50 minutes</u> writing your answers.
>
> - You'll be tested on <u>assessment objectives 1, 2, 3 and 4</u> in this section.
>
> Section B (writing) has two questions, worth <u>20 marks</u> each. You need to answer <u>both</u> questions:
>
> - You should spend about <u>30 minutes</u> on each question.
>
> - For each question, give yourself <u>5 minutes</u> to plan and <u>25 minutes</u> to write your answer.
>
> - This section will test <u>assessment objectives 5 and 6</u>.

PAPER 2

Both papers have the <u>same number</u> of marks, but paper 1 is worth <u>40%</u> of the GCSE and paper 2 is worth <u>60%</u>.

"How did you find the exam?" "It was just on the table..."

After the ten minutes of reading time, you've got just over a minute per mark for the reading questions in both exam papers. Stick to that rule and you'll have a good go at all the questions in the time you're given.

The Assessment Objectives

If you've got the basic structure covered, now's a good time to get your head around the sort of thing the examiners will be looking for in your answers — ladies and gentlemen, I give you the assessment objectives...

Each assessment objective refers to a different skill

1) The <u>assessment objectives</u> are the things that <u>Eduqas</u> say you need to <u>do</u> to get good marks in the exam.

2) They'll come in handy when you're working out what you need to do for <u>each question</u> (have a look back at p.1 to see which sections of the exams test which assessment objectives).

3) These exams test <u>assessment objectives 1 to 6</u>. Here's a brief description of each of them:

Assessment Objective 1

- <u>Pick out</u> and <u>understand</u> pieces of <u>explicit</u> and <u>implicit</u> information from the texts.
- <u>Collect</u> and <u>put together</u> information from different texts.

Explicit information is clearly written in the text. Implicit information isn't as obvious — you'll need to work it out from what is said in the text. See p.12.

Assessment Objective 2

- <u>Explain</u> how writers use <u>language</u> and <u>structure</u> to achieve their <u>purpose</u> and <u>influence</u> readers.
- Use <u>technical terms</u> to support your analysis of language and structure.

Assessment Objective 3

- <u>Identify</u> different writers' <u>ideas</u> and <u>perspectives</u>.
- <u>Compare</u> the <u>methods</u> used by different writers to convey their ideas.

Assessment Objective 4

- <u>Critically evaluate</u> texts, giving a <u>personal opinion</u> about how successful the writing is.
- Provide detailed <u>evidence</u> from the text to <u>support</u> your opinion.

Assessment Objective 5

- Write <u>clearly</u> and <u>imaginatively</u>, adapting your tone and style for various <u>purposes</u> and <u>audiences</u>.
- <u>Organise</u> your writing into a clear <u>structure</u>.

Assessment Objective 6

- Use a wide variety of <u>sentence structures</u> and <u>vocabulary</u>, so that your writing is <u>clear</u> and <u>purposeful</u>.
- Write <u>accurately</u>, paying particular attention to spelling, punctuation and grammar.

Understanding the assessment objectives is the key to success...

It's really important that you get to know these assessment objectives — they tell you what you need to do to get the maximum marks available. Next stop, world domination — if only you could do a GCSE in that...

Planning Answers

Now you know about what to expect from the exams, the next few pages will help you with the basics of how to answer the questions. First up, what to do before you start scribbling away at the answers...

Read the questions carefully and calmly

1) You should start each exam by spending about 10 minutes reading through the questions and the texts in Section A.

The exam texts might also be referred to as 'passages' or 'extracts'.

2) Always read the questions before the exam texts — that way, you'll know what to look out for.

3) Make sure you're clear about what the questions are asking you to do by underlining the key words.

A5. According to these two writers, why should people try to spend less?

4) Once you've read the questions, carefully read through the texts. It's a good idea to highlight key words or phrases in the texts that will help you to answer the questions — but don't spend ages doing this.

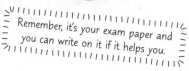

Remember, it's your exam paper and you can write on it if it helps you.

Jot down your main ideas before you start writing

1) Don't spend too much time planning. You don't need to write plans for the Section A reading questions, though it might help to quickly jot down some points and highlight the texts.

2) You should do plans for the Section B writing questions on both papers.

3) Don't go into too much detail — just get your main ideas down, and outline the structure of your answer.

B2. Your local council has made a proposal to fund the construction of new cycle routes in your area.

You have decided to write an article for your local newspaper to share your views on this proposal. You could write in favour or against this proposal.

Write a lively article for your local newspaper giving your views.

Make sure your points are linked to the question — think about purpose, form and audience.

Make sure you're clear which side you're arguing for before you start.

PLAN

Para 1 — Intro: proposal = positive step for our local community, we should be supporting more sustainable modes of transport.

Para 2 — Will improve environment — cycling more environmentally friendly than driving.

Para 3 — Cycling provides many health benefits, so general health of residents will improve.

Para 4 — Counter-argument: some say cycle routes too expensive. However, cycle routes will bring tourism — benefits to economy counteract cost.

Para 5 — Conc: The council should be supported in this initiative.

Briefly outline the focus of each paragraph.

To save time, write in note form.

A plan is like a nice hot water bottle...

... useful and comforting when you need it, but you don't need it all the time. You won't need to plan for every question, but you should make a brief plan for the writing questions in Section B of each paper.

P.E.E.D.

You can have loads of great ideas in your answers, but you won't get good marks unless you explain and develop them properly. That's where P.E.E.D. comes in — use it wisely my young apprentice...

P.E.E.D. stands for Point, Example, Explain, Develop

You don't need to use P.E.E.D. for short fact-finding questions.

To write good answers for the <u>longer reading questions</u>, you must do <u>four</u> things:

1) Make a <u>point</u> to answer the question you've been given.

2) Then give an <u>example</u> from the text (see page 5 for more on this).

3) After that, <u>explain</u> how your example backs up your point.

4) Finally, <u>develop</u> your point — this might involve things like saying what the <u>effect on the reader</u> is, saying what the <u>writer's intention</u> is or <u>linking</u> your point to another part of the text.

"That wasn't really the kind of back up I was hoping for..." thought the sergeant.

The <u>explanation</u> and <u>development</u> parts are very important. They're your chance to show that you <u>really understand</u> and have <u>thought about</u> the text. Here are a couple of <u>examples</u>:

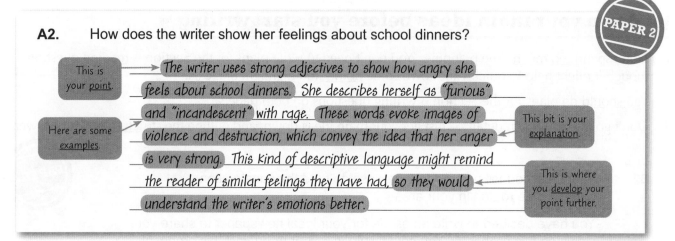

A2. How does the writer show her feelings about school dinners?

PAPER 2

This is your <u>point</u>. → The writer uses strong adjectives to show how angry she feels about school dinners. She describes herself as "furious" and "incandescent" with rage. These words evoke images of violence and destruction, which convey the idea that her anger is very strong. This kind of descriptive language might remind the reader of similar feelings they have had, so they would understand the writer's emotions better.

Here are some <u>examples</u>.

This bit is your <u>explanation</u>.

This is where you <u>develop</u> your point further.

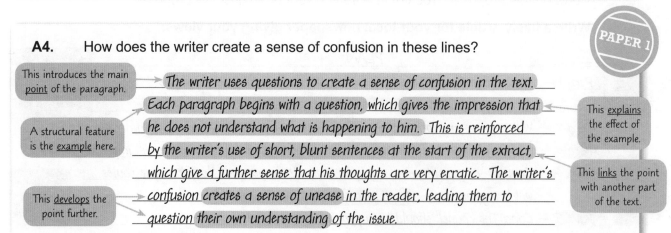

A4. How does the writer create a sense of confusion in these lines?

PAPER 1

This introduces the main <u>point</u> of the paragraph. → The writer uses questions to create a sense of confusion in the text. Each paragraph begins with a question, which gives the impression that he does not understand what is happening to him. This is reinforced by the writer's use of short, blunt sentences at the start of the extract, which give a further sense that his thoughts are very erratic. The writer's confusion creates a sense of unease in the reader, leading them to question their own understanding of the issue.

A structural feature is the <u>example</u> here.

This <u>develops</u> the point further.

This <u>explains</u> the effect of the example.

This <u>links</u> the point with another part of the text.

Would you like to share the joke with the rest of the class?

There are other versions of P.E.E.D., but they all mean similar things — P.E.E.R. (Point, Example, Explain, Relate), P.E.E.C.E. (Point, Example, Explain, Compare, Explore). I just chose P.E.E.D. because it tickles me...

Using Examples

This page has some nifty tips about the first 'E' in P.E.E.D. — giving examples to back up your points.

Use details from the text to back up your points

1) Whenever you make a new <u>point</u>, you need to use short pieces of <u>evidence</u> from the text to <u>back it up</u>.

2) You should try to use a <u>mix</u> of different sorts of <u>evidence</u>.

3) If you're using <u>quotes</u>, try to keep them <u>short</u>. It'll really impress the examiner if you <u>embed</u> them in a sentence, like this:

> The writer refers to the situation as "indefensible", suggesting that he is extremely critical of the way it has been handled.

Using short embedded quotes like this lets you combine the 'example' and 'explain' parts of P.E.E.D. in one sentence.

4) <u>Paraphrased details</u> from the text also work well as examples. You just need to describe one of the <u>writer's techniques</u>, or one of the <u>text's features</u>, in your own words, like this:

> The writer begins the paragraph with a rhetorical question that emphasises her feelings of disgust.

5) Here are a couple of <u>examples</u> to show you how to work your evidence into your answer:

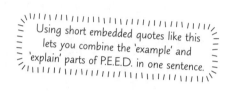

A2. How does the writer show the power of the fire?

The writer uses a mixture of linguistic devices to demonstrate the immense power of the fire. At the start of the extract, he paints a vivid picture of the fire as a "pageant" of colour. He then uses a metaphor to equate the destructive power of the fire with that of a beast that is tearing down the workshop and "devouring" it. All of these images make the fire seem impressive and potent.

Embedding short quotes will help your answer to flow smoothly.

Your example could just be a description of one of the writer's techniques.

A6. Both of these texts are about international travel. Compare the following:
- the writers' attitudes to international travel;
- how they get across their arguments.

The author of the newspaper article has a very negative attitude towards international travel. In her opening paragraph, she uses a long sentence that is packed with negative verbs and adjectives, including "delayed" and "dreary", to convey the hassle of long-distance travelling and to make the reader feel weary. By contrast, the author of the letter demonstrates a much more positive attitude. She opens her letter with the short but decisive sentence, "The journey was a perfect joy!", which sounds energetic and cheerful.

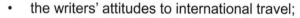

Try to include a good balance of quotes and references to the text.

If you need to use a longer quote, make sure you copy it correctly and use the correct punctuation.

Always make sure I've P.E.E.D. on my work... can I quote you on that?

Backing up your points with evidence from the text is a sure-fire way to impress the examiners. Then, you just need to explain the evidence and develop your point, and you'll be well on your way to P.E.E.D. perfection.

Section One — Exam Basics

Writing Well

A big chunk of the marks in these exams are for how you write rather than what you write. The next two pages will give you tips on how to write well for the longer reading questions on both papers.

Keep your writing formal but interesting

1) For these exams, it's important that you write in Standard English.

2) Standard English is the version of English that most people think is 'correct'. There are a few simple rules that you can follow to make sure you're writing in Standard English:

- Avoid using informal words and phrases (e.g. putting 'like' after sentences).

- Avoid using slang or local dialect words that some people might not understand.

- Avoid using clichés (words and phrases that are so commonly used that they've lost their effect) like 'at the end of the day'.

- Use correct spelling, punctuation and grammar (have a look at pages 10-11).

3) You should also try to make your writing as engaging as possible by using things like varied sentence lengths and interesting vocabulary. For example, avoid using unimaginative words such as 'nice' or 'good' — try to use other adjectives like 'charming' or 'admirable' instead.

Use clear explaining words and phrases

1) You should use explaining words and phrases to make your answers easy to follow.

| This signifies that... | This highlights the fact that... | This image reflects... |

| This is reminiscent of... | Furthermore... | This continues the idea of... |

2) Using words and phrases like these makes your writing sound more professional.

3) They're also really useful when it comes to P.E.E.D. (see page 4). They help you to link the explanation and development parts of your answer to your main point.

4) Here's an example of how to use explaining words and phrases to improve your answer:

A6. Both of these texts are about volunteering. Compare the following:
- the writers' attitudes to volunteering;
- how they get across their arguments.

> Start your paragraph with a new point, and back it up with evidence from the text. Then, explain how this evidence supports your point.

The writer of the magazine article uses a list of verbs ("giving, helping and sharing") to show that volunteering programmes are beneficial; the verbs are all positive, which highlights the fact that the author supports volunteering. The use of a list suggests that volunteering has a variety of benefits, which continues the idea that young people should do more to help others. Furthermore, it has a persuasive effect on the reader, making them feel that they should get involved in charity work.

> Use explaining words and phrases to show that you've developed your point.

> This phrase links the explanation to the rest of the point.

> This develops the point by showing its effect on the reader.

Section One — Exam Basics

Writing Well

Use paragraphs to structure your answer

1) You need to <u>organise</u> your points <u>clearly</u> and <u>link</u> them together
   — to do that you need to write in <u>paragraphs</u>.

2) You can use different paragraph <u>structures</u> to organise your points in different ways. For example:

> • You could write a paragraph for every <u>point</u> you want to make, and each paragraph could have a <u>P.E.E.D.</u> structure (see page 4).
>
> • You could make two points that <u>contrast</u> or <u>agree</u> with each other within a paragraph — this can be useful when <u>comparing</u> two texts.
>
> • You could make one point and <u>link</u> together lots of <u>examples</u> with <u>different</u> explanations within a paragraph.

> However you structure your paragraphs, make sure you include all the parts of P.E.E.D. in your answer.

3) <u>Linking</u> your paragraphs together <u>smoothly</u> makes your writing sound <u>confident</u> and <u>considered</u>. You could use linking words like these to help you do this:

| However... | In contrast... | On the other hand... | Equally... |
| In the same way... | In addition... | Alternatively... | Conversely... |

4) Take a look at the answer below for an <u>example</u> of how to use <u>paragraphs</u> effectively:

PAPER 1

A4. How does the writer make these lines sombre and tense?

> The writer uses a particular range of negative vocabulary to create a sombre, tense mood in the extract. Adjectives like "dismal" and "bleak", as well as verbs like "creaked" and "yawned", seem to build up and gradually make the reader feel more melancholy and unnerved. They give the sense that something bad is about to happen.
>
> Although the narrator's use of particular adjectives and verbs is important, it's not the only way in which the writer uses language to create a tense mood. Later in the extract, the writer also uses personification as a method of creating mood. He focuses specifically on the weather, bringing the rain and fog to life in order to create an eerie atmosphere. The personification of the rain as "stealthy" makes it seem menacing, whilst the image of it knocking "furtively" at the door adds to this mysterious atmosphere and makes the reader feel worried about what is going to happen next.
>
> In the same way, the writer also uses onomatopoeia, like the rain's "unsettling pattering" and the hedge's "rustling", to reinforce the tense mood of the piece.

The beginning of a paragraph needs to show what the paragraph is about. Try to link it to the key words in the question.

This is a new point, so it's in a new paragraph.

Use linking words and phrases to show that you are introducing a comparison or contrast with a previous paragraph.

You could link a new paragraph with a previous paragraph.

This answer fully develops each new point, covering all the different parts of P.E.E.D.

Make sure your answer is a model of structural perfection...

... and I'm not talking about cheekbones. Organise your ideas into paragraphs, and use the phrases on this page to link them together smoothly. A clear structure will show the examiner that you've thought about your answer.

Reading with Insight

To get the top grades, you need to show that you can 'read with insight' — you've got to make it clear that you've worked out what the text is saying beyond the blatantly obvious. Think of it like detective work, my dear Watson...

You need to look beyond what's obvious

1) You may understand the <u>facts</u> a writer gives you, but you'll need to write about <u>more</u> than just those facts in your answers.

2) You can show <u>insight</u> if you work out what the writer's <u>intentions</u> are and how they want the reader to <u>feel</u>.

3) Here are a couple of <u>examples</u> of the kinds of things you could write:

> Looking beyond what's obvious will help you to make sure you've done the 'D' part of P.E.E.D. — look back at p.4 for more on this.

The rhetorical questions make the reader doubt whether homework is a good thing. The writer seems to want to make readers feel guilty.

Think about the reasons <u>why</u> the writer has included certain features — show you've understood their <u>intended effect</u> on the reader.

There is a strong sense that the writer is suffering after the loss of his friend. Perhaps the writer felt he needed to make sure the memory of his friend was kept alive.
You could comment on the writer's <u>attitude</u> and <u>why</u> you think they chose to write the piece.

Show you've thought about the writer's intentions

A5. "In the last nine lines of this passage, the writer encourages the reader to view Lilian as an unlikeable character."

To what extent do you agree with this view?

> Dylan glowered across the table at Lilian. She was composed and collected, her pointed, reptilian features gathered into an expression of infuriating complacency; as he watched, a smug smile flickered at the edges of her mouth. She knew she had won.
>
> There hadn't even been a discussion. Lilian had been cool and emotionless, the picture of relaxed indifference. Her cruel blow, calculated to achieve maximum damage with minimum effort, had been delivered with the sniper-like accuracy that Dylan had always known she was capable of. Reeling from the shock of her abrupt revelation, Dylan barely had time to collect himself before the others had arrived.

Always show how your interpretation is based on the text.

Try to offer an alternative interpretation that goes beyond what is obvious in the text.

I agree that Lilian is portrayed as an unlikeable character in this extract. She is depicted as "smug" and she appears to be gloating. However, even though the writer is using the third-person, he is still showing us Lilian from Dylan's perspective. He has clearly been offended by her and so is biased against her. Some readers might side with Dylan against Lilian, finding her arrogant and malicious. Having said that, other readers might suspect that Dylan's pride has been wounded, and he is being overly harsh on Lilian as a result. Personally, I think the writer is using this description of Lilian to influence the reader's opinion of both her and Dylan by demonstrating that they both have flaws.

Try to pick out how the writer has made you feel like this.

Show you've thought about what the writer is trying to achieve beyond the obvious.

Reading with Insight

Inference means working things out from clues

1) Writers don't usually make things obvious — but you can use <u>evidence</u> from the text to make an <u>inference</u> about what the writer <u>really</u> wants us to think.

2) You need to analyse <u>details</u> from the text to show what they <u>reveal</u> about the writer's intentions:

> *The writer uses words like "endless" and "unoriginal", which imply that he did not enjoy the film.*   The writer's <u>language</u> indicates their <u>emotions</u> and <u>attitude</u>.

> *The writer sounds sarcastic when she calls the contestants "the finest brains the country could scrape together".*   The writer will often use <u>tone</u> (see page 25) to <u>imply</u> what they really mean — look out for <u>sarcasm</u> or <u>bias</u>.

3) You could use <u>phrases</u> like these to show that you've made an <u>inference</u>:

> The writer gives a sense of...   The writer appears to be...   This suggests that...

Try to read between the lines

PAPER 2

A2. How does the writer try to persuade us that the Internet has had a negative impact on our lives?

> In today's world we are plagued by information. Gone are the days of blissful ignorance; instead we inhabit an era of awareness, where the invention of the Internet has brought the sum total of the world's knowledge to our fingertips. We are gluttons for information, and yet the immediate availability of this information has irrevocably extinguished the dying embers of our curiosity. No longer do we wonder about anything, we simply look it up. I am willing to concede that the Internet might be one of man's greatest inventions, but hey, so was the atomic bomb.

Use words like 'seemingly' to show that you've thought about the meaning of the text beyond the obvious.

Analyse the writer's individual word choices for clues about how they try to affect the reader (see pages 27-28).

The writer makes some seemingly positive claims about the Internet: she grandly asserts that it has created "an era of awareness" that has brought all the world's knowledge "to our fingertips". However, the tone of the text suggests that she wants the reader to see this as a bad thing. She uses negative words like "plagued" and "gluttons" to make the availability of information seem dangerous and excessive. She also describes the Internet as "one of man's greatest inventions", but the subsequent comparison to "the atomic bomb" indicates her sarcastic tone, and invites the reader to view the invention of the Internet as a destructive event.

Your inferences could be based on the general feeling you get from reading the text.

Writers often use sarcasm to try to persuade the reader to agree with them (see page 34).

Make sure you're reading with insight of a cup of tea...

Keep an eye out for any clues that might reveal how the writer has crafted their text to have a particular effect on the reader — they've certainly got a few tricks up their sleeves, these pesky writers.

Spelling, Punctuation and Grammar

A great way to make sure you grab a few easy marks in these exams is to use correct spelling, punctuation and grammar, or SPaG for short. These pages should help you to avoid the most common SPaG errors...

SPaG is especially important for the writing questions

1) It's important that you use correct spelling, punctuation and grammar in all of your answers.

2) However, it's particularly important for the writing questions (Section B on both papers), as they will test your ability to write accurately and clearly — which includes good SPaG.

3) Here are some tips to help keep your writing as accurate as possible.

Spelling

1) Avoid common spelling mistakes, like 'their', 'they're' and 'there' or 'where', 'were' and 'wear'.

2) Remember that 'affect' is a verb, e.g. 'the simile affects the mood of the text', but 'effect' is a noun, e.g. 'the interruption has a shocking effect on the reader'.

3) Always write words out in full — avoid abbreviations like 'etc.' and 'e.g.', and don't use text speak.

4) Make sure any technical terms, like 'metaphor' or 'onomatopoeia', are spelt correctly.

5) Make sure any information taken from the extract, such as the writer's name, is spelt correctly.

Punctuation

1) Make sure you've used full stops at the end of sentences and question marks at the end of questions.

2) Use commas to separate items in a list or when you've used more than one adjective.

3) Use a comma when you use a joining word like 'and', 'so' or 'but' to link two points together. E.g. 'Jeremy says he isn't bothered by Mandy's behaviour, but his body language suggests otherwise'.

4) You should also use a pair of commas to separate extra information in a sentence. E.g. 'Ranjita, who is much calmer than Ashanti, does not respond to her father's taunting'.

5) Don't confuse colons and semi-colons.

   - Colons can be used to introduce a list or if you want to add a piece of information that explains your sentence.

   - Semi-colons can separate longer phrases in a list, or they can be used to join two sentences together — as long as both sentences are about the same thing and make sense on their own.

Grammar

1) Don't change tenses in your writing by mistake. If you're writing about a text in Section A, always use the present tense, e.g. 'The writer uses alliteration to make Jane seem angry'.

2) Don't use double negatives, e.g. 'There wasn't no reason' should be 'There wasn't any reason'.

3) Remember 'it's' (with an apostrophe) is short for 'it is' or 'it has'. 'Its' (without an apostrophe) means 'belonging to it', e.g. 'The dog found its bone'.

4) Never write 'should of' — it's always 'should have', 'would have', 'could have'.

5) Start a new paragraph for each new point. Show that it's a new paragraph by starting a new line and leaving a gap or indent before you start writing.

Spelling, Punctuation and Grammar

Check over your work when you've finished

1) Try to leave a few minutes at the <u>end</u> of the exams to <u>check</u> your work.

2) There might not be <u>time</u> to check everything thoroughly. Look for the <u>most obvious</u> spelling, punctuation and grammar mistakes.

3) Start by checking your answers to the <u>writing questions</u> (Section B on both papers), as these are the ones where you get the <u>most marks</u> for accuracy.

4) Here are some tips for <u>correcting</u> any mistakes that you find:

- If you find a <u>spelling mistake</u>, put <u>brackets</u> around the word, <u>cross it out</u> neatly with <u>two lines</u> through it and write the correction <u>above</u>.

- If you've written something which isn't clear, put an <u>asterisk</u> (*) at the end of the sentence. Put another asterisk at the end of your work, and write what you mean beside it.

- If you realise you should have started a <u>new paragraph</u>, put // to show where it <u>starts</u> and write "(para)" in the margin.

- If you find you've <u>missed out</u> a word or two, put a "∧" where the words should go, then write them in <u>above</u> the line.

Make corrections as neatly as possible

PAPER 1

SECTION B: WRITING

(a) Write a story which begins: *The air was stiflingly hot...*

The air was stiflingly hot. Monica could feel a dewy coating of sweat materialising on her clammy skin as she ∧(reclined) in the middle of the park. She kept one eye on the romantic novel that she held in her hand, and the other peering through the summer haze at Ollie as he charged around the open space with the other boys. It was difficult to concentrate on anything in this weather; Monica had felt harassed and tormented by the relentless, sweltering heat all week. // Her mind wandered from the novel, and she began to ponder the evening ahead. She had originally planned to wear her comfortable but contemporary denim skirt with her favourite brown boots. This was certainly not an option in this weather though. She would have to think of something else. Perhaps the floral dress that she had worn last summer to Rachel's wedding would work.

Suddenly, her rambling mind was brought back to reality with a start. A loud scream resonated around the park. Monica jumped to her (feet) *feet* and began running.

(para)

Make sure you use semi-colons and colons correctly.

Commas can be used between two adjectives or before a joining word that is being used to link two points.

Think carefully about how you link your paragraphs.

Accuracy is important, but don't let it put you off using a wide range of vocabulary and sentence structures.

Be careful with your tenses — make sure they're consistent.

Correct any mistakes clearly and neatly.

Follow these simple instructions to produce a SPaG-tastic answer...

Getting your SPaG right is super important, but don't let it put you off using a wide range of vocabulary and sentence types. You need to be able to write accurately, but also use your imagination, in order to do well.

Information and Ideas

These two pages will help you to deal with assessment objective 1 (see p.2). This page is about picking out information from a text, and the next page is about summarising information from two different texts.

Information and ideas can be explicit or implicit

1) The first thing you need to be able to do in order to <u>analyse</u> a text is to <u>understand</u> the basic things it's <u>telling you</u>.

2) This will help you to pick up some <u>easy marks</u> for <u>Section A</u> in both exam papers.

3) The information and ideas you need to pick out will either be <u>explicit</u> or <u>implicit</u>.

4) <u>Explicit</u> information is <u>clearly written</u> in the text.

> *Last weekend, it rained a lot.* ⟹ The text states that it rained, so we <u>know</u> that it rained. We also know <u>how much</u> it rained — "a lot."

"It rained HOW much?"

5) <u>Implicit</u> information needs a little more <u>detective work</u> — you'll need to work it out from what is said in the text.

> *The castle was dark, decrepit and freezing cold.* ⟹ In this sentence, it is <u>implied</u> that the author doesn't like the castle very much, but this isn't stated outright.

Underline the relevant facts as you read the text

PAPER 1

Read lines 1-9.

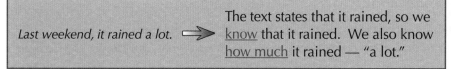

A1.   List **five** reasons why Brian disliked going to school.

If a question asks you to 'list' something, all you need to do is find the information in the text. You don't need to analyse it at all.

The facts that you use in your answer must come from the part of the text mentioned in the question.

> With a wry smile, Brian thought back to the <u>disgusting canteen food</u>, the <u>freezing classrooms</u> and the <u>awful teachers</u> he'd endured at school.
>
> St Mary's had been closer to Brian's house, but that had been an all-girls school. This meant that every morning Brian had been forced to withstand the torment of a <u>fifty-minute bus journey</u> across town to Beeches Hall — the boys' school. This bus journey was made all the worse for the driver: a peculiar, <u>unpleasant man</u> with a severely erratic driving style. Brian had been <u>constantly queasy</u>, which had given the bullies on the bus even more reason to <u>tease him</u>.

As you read the relevant part of the text, underline the facts that you could use to answer the question.

Write down your facts as concisely as you can.

 The food was "disgusting".

The classrooms were very cold.

The teachers were "awful".

The bus driver was "unpleasant".

The journey to school made Brian travel-sick.

This fact isn't explicitly written in the text, but it is implied.

You can paraphrase parts of the text...

... or you can quote directly from it. Just don't copy out big chunks from the text — that could lose you marks.

Information and Ideas

You'll also need to summarise information

1) In Section A of paper 2, you will be asked to pick out information and ideas on the <u>same topic</u> from two <u>different texts</u>.

2) You then need to write a <u>summary</u> about the <u>topic</u> — a piece of writing that <u>combines</u> the ideas from both texts, but is written using your <u>own words</u>.

3) Summaries need to be <u>concise</u> — try to sum up <u>all</u> the information you've gathered in as <u>few sentences</u> as possible.

4) For summarising questions, you <u>don't</u> need to <u>compare</u> the two texts — you just need to <u>explain</u> what they say about the <u>topic</u> in the question.

5) Even though you're using your own words, you still need to <u>back up</u> everything you write with a range of <u>examples</u> from both texts.

Conciseness had never been Gemma's strong point.

Questions that ask you to summarise will usually be worth <u>fewer</u> marks than questions that ask you to compare the texts.

Collect information from both texts

PAPER 2

A5. According to these two writers, why should people avoid travelling?

This question asks you to summarise what the texts say about why people shouldn't travel.

21st-century newspaper

In general, travelling is the last way I want to spend my time: the stress of catching connecting planes or trains gives me a coronary, and I suffer from chronic, restless boredom when forced to sit down for long periods of time. The environmental costs of travel also turn me off the idea — long-haul flights release tonnes of harmful carbon emissions into the atmosphere.

19th-century letter

The journey was simply dreadful, my dear Louisa. I know it is not becoming of a lady to say such things, but the jolting of the carriage has left my poor nerves shot to pieces; a truly alarming experience. And yet somehow so tedious, too — I should think that there is no activity more monotonous than the act of transporting oneself from one destination to another.

Combine evidence from both texts to make your answer as concise as possible.

The writers suggest that you should avoid travelling because it can be both stressful and monotonous: in the newspaper article, the writer mentions that journeys can involve "stress" and "boredom", and the writer of the letter mentions the effect of travel on her "nerves", as well as how "tedious" she finds travelling. In the modern age, there are also environmental reasons not to travel, as the writer of the newspaper article explains: long-haul flights release "tonnes of harmful carbon emissions" into the air.

Use key words to show the examiner that you've understood the question.

Answer the question in your own words, then back your points up with evidence from the texts.

In summary, learn these pages for top marks in the exams...

When you're summarising, mention the explicit ideas that pop up in the texts, but don't be afraid to dig deep and write about any implicit ideas you spot — they'll help you craft a really perceptive summary of the texts.

Audience

In the exams, you'll need to think about the audience — the intended readers of the text.

Writers aim their work at general or specific audiences

1) The writer will always have a group of people in mind when they write — this is their audience.

2) The audience of a text can be quite general, e.g. adults, or more specific, e.g. parents with children under the age of 3.

3) Some texts will have more than one audience, e.g. children's books will try to appeal to the kids who read them, but also to the parents who will buy them.

How about this one, Jonny? 'Dictionary' by Colin English. Sounds like a ripping yarn.

Look for clues about the target audience

1) Sometimes you can work out who the target audience is by the text's content (subject matter):

This latest model is a beautiful car. Its impressive engine can send you shooting from 0-60 mph in less than 8 seconds. This text is clearly aimed at someone who's interested in high-performance cars.

2) The vocabulary (choice of words) can tell you about the target audience, e.g. about the age group:

Today, we witnessed a discussion on fox-hunting. As one can imagine, this issue, although it has been debated for many years, still managed to elicit mixed emotions from all concerned. The sophisticated vocabulary, like 'elicit', rather than 'bring out', and the complex sentences show that this text is aimed at adults.

Dungeon Killer 3 is the hottest new game of the year! There are 52 awesome levels and 6 cool new characters — don't miss out on the wildest gaming experience of your life! This one uses modern slang and simple sentences, so it's clear that this text is aimed at younger people.

3) The language can also give you clues about the target audience's level of understanding:

The object of a game of football is to get the ball in the opposing team's goal. Sounds easy, but the other team has the same thing in mind. Also, there are eleven players on the other team trying to stop you. The simple, general explanations in this text show that it's written for people who don't know much about football.

The next hole was a par 3 and I hit my tee shot directly onto the green. Sadly, my putting let me down badly, and I ended up getting a bogey. The technical vocabulary here shows that this is for people who know quite a bit about golf.

And now we'll take any questions from the audience...

You need to work out who the intended audience of a text is so that you can discuss the writer's purpose, the techniques they use and how successful they are. Keep the target audience in mind throughout your answer.

Writer's Purpose

Writers rarely write something just for the benefit of their health. Unless it's a letter to their doctor...

There are four common purposes of writing

1) The <u>purpose</u> of a text is the <u>reason</u> that it's been written — what the writer is <u>trying to do</u>.

2) Most texts are written for <u>one</u> of these reasons:

To Argue or Persuade
- They give the writer's <u>opinion</u>.
- They get the reader to <u>agree</u> with them.

To Advise
- They <u>help</u> the reader to <u>do something</u>.
- They give <u>instructions</u> on what to do.

To Inform
- They <u>tell</u> the reader about something.
- They help the reader to increase their <u>understanding</u> of a subject.

To Entertain
- They are <u>enjoyable</u> to read.
- They make the reader <u>feel</u> something.

3) Lots of texts have <u>more than one</u> purpose, though. E.g. a biographical text could be written to both <u>inform</u> and <u>entertain</u> its audience.

4) In the exams, read the texts carefully and make sure that you think about <u>what</u> the writers are trying to <u>achieve</u> (and <u>how</u> they're achieving it).

Pages 16-19 tell you how to spot a text's purpose, and how you can discuss this in the exams.

5) Look out for super helpful exam questions that actually <u>tell you</u> the writer's purpose. E.g. if the question asks you about how the writer uses language to <u>influence</u> the reader, you know it's about <u>persuading</u>.

Purpose is more obvious in non-fiction texts

1) The purpose of most <u>non-fiction</u> texts is usually quite <u>obvious</u>. For example:

If a speech is trying to <u>argue</u> a particular point of view, the writer might make this very <u>clear</u> to make the argument more <u>powerful</u>.

2) Look out for texts where it might be <u>less obvious</u>, though. For example:

A <u>magazine article</u> is primarily written to <u>entertain</u> its audience, so it might use a <u>chatty</u> tone to engage the reader. This might make it <u>less obvious</u> that it's also trying to <u>argue</u> a particular point of view.

Barry's porpoise in life had always been to entertain.

3) A piece of fiction's most obvious purpose is to <u>entertain</u>, but writers sometimes use entertainment to achieve <u>another purpose</u>.

Lots of fiction texts are <u>entertaining</u> stories on the surface, but they can contain <u>another message</u>. The writer might want to <u>argue</u> their own point of view or <u>inform</u> the reader about something.

This page was no accident — I wrote it on purpose...

So purpose can be a little harder to figure out than you'd think. If there's more than one purpose to a text, write about them both. And if you can write about how one purpose is used to achieve another, even better.

Informative Texts

I don't want to blow your mind or anything, but this page about informative texts is *itself* an informative text.

Informative writing tells you something

1) When writing an informative text, the writer's aim is to pass on <u>knowledge</u> to the reader as <u>clearly</u> and <u>effectively</u> as possible.

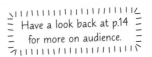
Have a look back at p.14 for more on audience.

2) They will adapt their <u>language</u> to match their intended <u>audience</u>, e.g. they <u>might</u> need to write for different <u>age groups</u>, or for people with different <u>levels of understanding</u>.

3) Purely informative texts will present information in a <u>balanced</u> and <u>factual</u> way. They will contain lots of <u>facts</u> and <u>figures</u>, but no <u>opinions</u>.

4) Some informative texts might also be <u>arguing</u> a particular viewpoint, though. For example:

Many newspapers <u>carefully pick</u> information that supports a particular political party. Even though a newspaper article may not say outright what its opinion is, it can still be <u>biased</u>.

Bias is when a piece of writing is influenced by the opinion of its author — see page 36.

Read the passage carefully

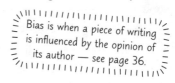
PAPER 2

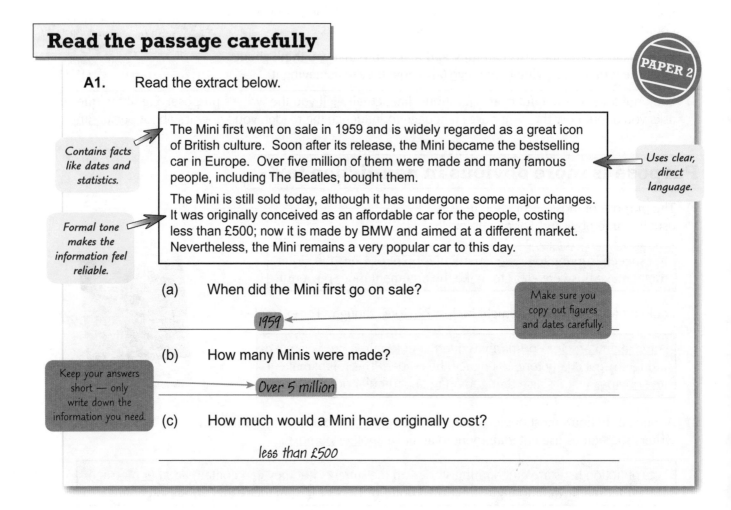

A1. Read the extract below.

The Mini first went on sale in 1959 and is widely regarded as a great icon of British culture. Soon after its release, the Mini became the bestselling car in Europe. Over five million of them were made and many famous people, including The Beatles, bought them.

The Mini is still sold today, although it has undergone some major changes. It was originally conceived as an affordable car for the people, costing less than £500; now it is made by BMW and aimed at a different market. Nevertheless, the Mini remains a very popular car to this day.

Contains facts like dates and statistics.

Uses clear, direct language.

Formal tone makes the information feel reliable.

(a) When did the Mini first go on sale?

    1959

Make sure you copy out figures and dates carefully.

(b) How many Minis were made?

    Over 5 million

Keep your answers short — only write down the information you need.

(c) How much would a Mini have originally cost?

    less than £500

You were promised informative, and you got informative...

Yes indeedio, there's plenty of information here to keep you occupied. You need to be able to recognise informative writing and explain how it's being used. And if the information is biased, be sure to point it out.

Entertaining Texts

After an informative text about informative texts, here's a (hopefully) entertaining text about entertaining texts.

Entertaining writing aims to be enjoyable to read

1) Entertaining writing is the sort of thing you'd read for <u>pleasure</u>, e.g. literary fiction.

2) Unlike informative texts, they contain <u>few facts</u>. Instead, they try to make you <u>feel</u> something, like <u>scared</u>, <u>excited</u>, or <u>amused</u>.

3) Entertaining writing is often very <u>descriptive</u>, and uses <u>narrative techniques</u> to make texts more enjoyable to read (see p.37-38).

4) Writers also use <u>structural techniques</u> to create entertaining texts (see p.39-43). E.g. lots of <u>short</u>, <u>punchy</u> sentences can be used to make a text feel more <u>exciting</u>.

Tony's bank statement was lacking in entertaining passages.

> Writers might use entertaining writing to <u>engage</u> a reader when they have <u>another</u> purpose in mind. E.g. travel books are <u>entertaining non-fiction</u>, which are also <u>informative</u>.

Think about what makes the text entertaining

PAPER 1

A4. How does the writer make these lines exciting and tense?

> He could feel the power of the bike humming beneath him as they both hurtled along. They were an elegant couple skimming the dance floor, whirling past plodding onlookers in their graceless automobiles, twisting around sweeping corners with effortless precision and darting along endless straights as they pushed each other on towards the inevitable conclusion. The bike hit the wall with all its hulking force.

Lots of creative vocabulary makes the text more interesting.

The text uses imagery to make the description come to life.

Different sentence lengths give the text an interesting structure.

In order to build excitement for the reader, the writer uses an extended metaphor that personifies the bike as a dance partner. The bike and the rider become an "elegant couple" whose movements contrast with the "plodding" cars. The writer uses a long sentence to develop this metaphor and build drama. This lengthy second sentence contains several verbs that are related to dancing and speed, such as "whirling" and "darting". The cumulative effect of these verbs makes the reader feel tense. It is as if the sentence is rushing and building towards a conclusion. The writer then disperses this tension with the final short sentence. The phrase "hit the wall" is very blunt, and contrasts to the preceding build-up, adding to the shock and impact of the conclusion.

Use key words from the question to keep your answer focused.

You need to use technical terms.

Try to identify how the writer uses different parts of speech.

You should analyse the language at both word and sentence level.

Write about the writer's intentions and the effects of their language on the reader.

Fortunately, I know a thing or two about entertaining writing...

Entertaining writing really helps to keep readers interested. So even if a writer's main purpose is to inform, argue, persuade or advise, they might still want to make their writing entertaining so the reader enjoys it.

Texts that Argue or Persuade

So many texts are written to argue. If only there was some way we could persuade them all to just get along...

Arguing and persuading are similar

1) When people write to <u>argue</u>, they want to make the reader <u>agree</u> with their <u>opinion</u>. They use <u>clear</u> and <u>forceful</u> language to get their points across, and they might use <u>facts and figures</u> to back up points.

2) <u>Persuasive</u> writing often tries to get the reader to <u>do something</u>, such as support a charity. It does this with techniques including <u>emotive language</u> that aims to make the reader <u>sympathise</u> with their cause.

3) A writer might also try to persuade the reader by presenting an <u>opinion</u> as if it were <u>definitely true</u>:

> *It is clear that this is a good school, and that people who attend it do well.* This writer uses the phrase 'It is clear' to make their <u>opinion</u> sound like <u>fact</u>. This can make the writing sound more <u>informative</u>, when actually it's <u>persuasive</u>.

4) When writing to argue or persuade, writers often use <u>rhetorical devices</u> such as <u>hyperbole</u>, <u>repetition</u> or <u>rhetorical questions</u> (see p.35).

Explain the effects of the writer's choice of language

PAPER 2

A2. David Barowsky is trying to persuade us to eat breakfast. How does he try to do this?

WHY BOTHER WITH BREAKFAST?

David Barowsky, *nutritional analyst*

The writer uses statements to make their point clearly and forcefully.

Uses rhetorical questions.

Eating breakfast improves mental and physical performance. This is a well-known and incontrovertible fact. And yet 20 million of us Britons regularly skip this essential refuelling opportunity. Why is this the case? Are we too busy commuting, getting the kids ready for school, blow-drying our hair? Do you often feel frantic and harassed in the morning? Well, the time has come to change your ways. Allowing your kids to skip breakfast is reckless and irresponsible. You are not providing them with the energy they need to face the day.

Facts and figures are used to back up their argument.

Addresses the reader directly using the pronoun 'you'.

The writer captures the reader's attention by using an alliterative rhetorical question as a title. Barowsky then immediately, and assertively, answers the question in the first line. This makes the writer sound both authoritative and knowledgeable, so readers are more likely to trust him and follow his advice to "bother with breakfast".
Barowsky also uses the personal pronouns "you" and "we" to establish a connection with the reader, whilst powerful adjectives like "reckless" and "irresponsible" encourage an emotional response. This personal connection gives the writer a platform from which he can challenge the reader's actions and persuade them to agree with his views.

Try to use varied vocabulary to describe the effects of the writer's language on the reader.

Try to use technical terms wherever you can.

Comment on the effects of individual words.

Persuasive texts are great, don't you agree? I knew you would...

If a writer is trying to argue a point or persuade you to do something, they're trying to make you see things from their point of view. It'll be one-sided, with carefully chosen evidence that supports their point of view.

Texts that Advise

Good advice is hard to come by these days, but don't panic — there's no shortage of it here.

Writing to advise sounds clear and calm

1) When writing to <u>advise</u>, writers want their readers to <u>follow their suggestions</u>.

2) The tone will be <u>calm</u> and <u>less emotional</u> than writing that argues or persuades.

3) The advice will usually be <u>clear</u> and <u>direct</u>. For example, it might use:

- <u>Vocabulary</u> that matches the audience's <u>subject knowledge</u>.
- <u>Second person</u> pronouns (e.g. 'you') to make the advice feel <u>personal</u>.
- A <u>logical structure</u> that makes the advice <u>easy to follow</u>.

4) The register (see p.26) may be <u>formal</u>, e.g. in a letter from a solicitor offering legal advice, or <u>informal</u>, e.g. in a magazine advice column.

All Jemima needed was some clear advice from her stylist.

Writing to advise looks like this

A2. Claire Lohan is trying to advise us about pensions. How does she try to do this?

PAPER 2

YOUR MONEY MATTERS

Claire Lohan
independent financial advice

Uses questions the reader might have.

Which is the right pension for me?

Before you buy into a pension, you need to be sure that it's the right one for you — dropping out can mean that you lose a lot of the money you've already paid in.

Friendly warning.

Addresses the reader directly by using the pronoun 'you'.

You should look at the pension company's reputation, past results and penalties for changing schemes.

Uses specific details to give practical advice.

It might sound scary, but don't worry, you'll find the right one for you.

Reassures the reader.

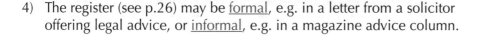

Remember to explain the effect of the quote.

The writer uses a friendly tone to communicate her advice in a clear, accessible way. When she advises, "you need to be sure", it sounds as if she is talking to a friend. This makes the reader more likely to take the advice, as it seems well-meant and helpful.

Develop the point — say why the writer has chosen this style.

Explain what sort of impression this type of language creates.

The language that the writer uses is specific but uncomplicated. She gives detailed advice, such as "look at the pension company's reputation, past results and penalties". This makes the writer seem well informed and knowledgeable. As a result, the reader is more likely to think that the advice is worthwhile, and act on it.

Stay focused on the writer's use of language.

Show that you know what effect it will have on the reader.

If you want my advice, I'd read through this page a couple of times

Texts that advise can be written for many different audiences, but a lot of the features will stay the same. Pay attention to whether the language is formal or informal — it'll vary depending on the subject and audience.

Writer's Viewpoint and Attitude

You always need to be aware of the writer's viewpoint, but it's especially important for paper 2.

Viewpoint and attitude are different to purpose

1) A writer's purpose is what they're trying to <u>do</u>, but their <u>viewpoint</u> (or attitude) is what they <u>think</u> about the <u>topics</u> that they're writing about.

2) You can work out what a writer's viewpoint might be by looking for clues in the <u>language</u>, <u>tone</u>, <u>style</u> and <u>content</u> of a text. For example:

> *I urge you to visit this truly unique and hidden valley — you must see such beautiful scenery at least once in your life.*

→ This text's <u>purpose</u> is to <u>persuade</u> its audience to visit a place. The <u>author's viewpoint</u> is their <u>belief</u> that the valley is beautiful and that it should be visited. The writer uses <u>emotive adjectives</u> and an <u>upbeat tone</u> to convey their viewpoint.

Use the writers' tone to make inferences about attitude

A6. Both of these texts are about etiquette. Compare the following:
- the writers' attitudes to etiquette;
- how they get across their arguments.

19th-century etiquette guide

The way you behave when out in society is paramount. It is essential that you show the highest level of social refinement possible. For example, if someone offers you their hand, take it. Always remove your hat when entering a building. Be punctual to all social events to which you are invited.

21st-century newspaper article

Anyone who's ever taken a ride on the London Underground will know that there are some real nuisances out there. All too often, I've seen people refusing to give their seat up to an elderly passenger. I mean, it's just common courtesy, isn't it? Is it really so difficult to just be a little more civil towards other people?

> Try to make your observations as perceptive as possible. Examiners will be really impressed if you can pick out subtle differences between the writers' attitudes.

> Use technical terms to discuss the different methods both writers use to convey their attitudes.

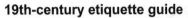

The authors of both sources largely agree that being polite is important. However, there are subtle differences in their attitudes. The 19th century writer uses a confident, assured tone, which is created by the use of imperative verbs such as "take" and "remove". They also give their advice using the pronoun "you", which makes the text sound more like a series of commands than a piece of advice. These things suggest that their ideas about "refinement" are very strict. By contrast, the newspaper article has a more relaxed tone. Rather than instructing the reader how to behave, the writer uses rhetorical questions to make the reader think about why people should be "more civil". This is possibly because the newspaper article is from the 21st century, whereas the etiquette guide was written in the 19th century, when etiquette was considered to be more important.

> This is a useful phrase to use when you're linking the two texts.

> Think about the reasons why their attitudes differ — think about when and why they were written.

These writers are just full of attitude...

Remember, you need to go beyond just <u>what</u> the writer's saying and think about <u>how</u> they're expressing their viewpoint. Even if two writers have the same opinion, one might express it more strongly than the other.

Section Two — Reading: Understanding Texts

Literature

In paper 1, you'll be given an extract from a piece of literature. So that's a snippet from a nice reading book — shame you won't be able to read it tucked up in bed with a lovely mug of hot chocolate though...

Literature entertains the reader

1) Literature, such as a novel or short story, is written to <u>entertain</u>. It might do this by affecting the reader's <u>emotions</u>, describing the <u>atmosphere</u> of a place, using an intriguing <u>structure</u> or developing the <u>personality</u> of a <u>character</u>.

2) All literature has a <u>narrator</u>. It's most often either a <u>first-person</u> (uses 'I' and 'we') or <u>third-person</u> (uses 'he', 'she' and 'they') narrator.

3) Literature uses lots of <u>descriptive</u> and <u>figurative</u> language (e.g. metaphors, similes, analogy and personification) to capture the reader's <u>imagination</u>.

4) Literature is also <u>structured</u> to interest the reader — texts will often build the <u>tension</u> towards a dramatic climax, or they might use <u>repetition</u> and varied <u>sentence structures</u> to change the <u>pace</u> of a text.

5) <u>Dialogue</u> is also often used to move the plot along and give insight into the <u>thoughts</u> and <u>feelings</u> of different characters.

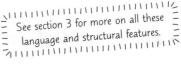

Gary thought he was entertaining, and a character, but no-one wanted to get to know his personality.

© Ljupco/iStockphoto.com

See section 3 for more on all these language and structural features.

Look closely at the language used in a text

PAPER 1

A3. What impressions do you get of the characters from these lines?

The adjective 'hurried' suggests that Edward is panicked.

This hints that Edward is worried or paranoid about something.

The writer uses Dorine's surroundings to tell the reader about her personality.

The narrative is third-person, so the reader can see from the perspective of both Edward and Dorine.

> Edward <mark>hurried</mark> down the dark, smog-filled alley. The place had become almost completely unrecognisable: the green fields he remembered from his childhood had long since been <mark>drowned</mark> in concrete. The alley became darker, and its bends and turns were increasingly disorientating. A creak. A whisper. <mark>Every noise put him on edge.</mark> <mark>But he pressed on.</mark>
>
> Eventually, Edward found himself at Dorine's lab. He walked in, stooping to avoid hitting his head on the low door frame. The lab was a large circular room; the walls were lined with <mark>hundreds of tattered books, and half-finished research papers</mark> lay strewn across the many desks.
>
> <mark>The books seemed to whisper to each other, as if disconcerted by the presence of an outsider. Edward felt as though they were watching him.</mark>
>
> Dorine was poring over some papers in front of her, and hadn't noticed that Edward had arrived. After a few moments, she looked up from her desk and saw Edward waiting. <mark>She could see</mark> the flicker of hope glimmering in his eyes — the hope that they might still be able to turn back the clock.
>
> "I'm afraid it's not looking good, <mark>Ed</mark>," Dorine murmured.
>
> *My God*, thought Edward. <mark>*How could we have let this happen?*</mark>

The use of the emotive verb 'drowned' shows that Edward doesn't like what's happened.

The fact that Edward carries on even though he is scared makes him seem determined.

Personification is used to show that Edward feels uncomfortable in the lab.

Using a shortened name implies that the two characters are well acquainted.

This rhetorical question suggests that Edward feels responsible for whatever's happened.

Narrative and descriptive techniques keep the reader interezzz...

There's a lot to learn on this page, but you're <u>always</u> going to have to answer some questions about a piece of literature. That means you're going to need to know all of this stuff really well — best get cracking then...

Literary Non-Fiction

You've had a look at some fiction on the previous page — now brace yourself for some non-fiction...

Literary non-fiction is entertaining but factual

1) Literary non-fiction texts use <u>literary styles</u> and <u>techniques</u>, but they are based on <u>facts</u> or <u>real events</u>.

2) Non-fiction texts such as <u>biographies</u>, <u>autobiographies</u>, and <u>travel writing</u> will often be written in a similar style to literary fiction.

3) They are written to <u>inform</u> the reader about something, but the writer uses a literary style to make it <u>entertaining</u> too. For example, they might use <u>descriptive</u> language and <u>dialogue</u> to make the information more <u>interesting</u> to the reader.

4) Literary non-fiction is almost always written in the <u>first person</u>, which adds a sense of <u>personality</u> to the text, helping to <u>engage</u> the reader.

5) Since you're only hearing <u>one person's</u> side of things, watch out for <u>bias</u> in literary non-fiction.

Have a look back at the previous page to remind yourself about literary style.

Literary non-fiction tries to engage the reader

PAPER 2

A4. What do you think and feel about the writer's views on the city of Paris?

Dearest reader — I wish today to impart to you some recollections of my summer spent in Paris, a city which over time has played host to a multitude of great thinkers and artists. A hundred years may have passed since the French Revolution, but Paris remains a shining beacon of revolutionary spirit.

The city of Paris has some spectacular specimens of architecture. One bright evening, I took a particularly enjoyable stroll down the Champs-Élysées, and was quite amazed by the stunning curvature of its Arc de Triomphe. The arch incited within me the strongest feelings of awe and wonderment; it is truly a structure built to inspire.

Paris has been ever-popular with the gentleman traveller, but this year the city captures one's imagination more than ever before, as it hosts the annual 'World's Fair'. There I saw many wonderful artefacts, including a magnificent replica of the Bastille, the famous site of the rebellion which began France's Revolution. The replica was incredibly lifelike, from the gloomy outer stonework to the banquet hall within.

Although the fortress was a thrilling diversion, it was far from the real star of the fair — that honour belonged to the newly-erected 'Eiffel Tower', said to be the largest building on Earth. The new tower amazed fair-goers with its enormous metallic form (although some were not altogether thrilled by its brash modernity). Whether one marvels at this remarkable feat of engineering, or recoils from its audacious magnitude, the new tower is assuredly a sight to behold.

This text uses a story-telling style and a first-person narrator to add personality — the writer is trying to engage and entertain the reader.

Imagery is used to convey the writer's admiration for the city.

The text uses lots of emotive adjectives to clearly show the writer's positive attitude towards Paris. Purely informative non-fiction wouldn't use adjectives like these.

The writer's description of their personal feelings helps the reader to engage with the text and understand the writer's views about Paris.

This sentence creates suspense by not revealing what the 'real star' is right away — the writer is essentially telling a story, so they try to create some tension for the reader.

We'll always have (a non-fiction text about) Paris...

You probably haven't had much contact with the phrase "literary non-fiction" before, but don't let the jargon fool you — it's just a category that describes any text that is factual, but is written in an entertaining way.

19th-Century Texts

In paper 2, you'll always be given a 19th-century non-fiction text to analyse. Chances are you weren't around much in those days, so this page should have some pretty useful information for you.

19th-century writing is often quite formal

1) 19th-century texts can sound a bit <u>different</u> to more modern texts, but you should still be able to <u>understand</u> what's going on.

2) A lot of the texts will use a more <u>formal register</u> (see p.26) than modern writing, even if the <u>audience</u> is quite <u>familiar</u> (see next page for an example of this).

3) The sentences may be <u>quite long</u> and the <u>word order</u> can sometimes be different to modern texts. Try not to worry about this — just <u>re-read</u> any sentences you can't make sense of at first. Here are a couple of examples:

> *Then, Albert being gone and we two left alone, Edward enquired as to whether I might accompany him on a stroll in the garden.*

> This sentence is written using a <u>formal</u> register, e.g. it uses 'enquired' instead of 'asked'. It might seem a bit <u>confusingly phrased</u> too, but 'Albert being gone and we two left alone' is just <u>another way</u> of saying 'Albert had gone and the two of us were left alone.'

> *I believe it necessary to abandon this foul enterprise.*

> Sometimes it can seem as if a word has been <u>missed out</u> — modern writers would probably put 'is' after 'it' in this sentence.

19th-century society was different to today

1) Knowing about 19th-century <u>society</u> will help you to <u>understand</u> the text better in the exam.

2) It will also help you to compare the <u>attitudes</u> of writers from different <u>time periods</u>, which you need to do in paper 2.

Social Class

*   Early 19th-century society was <u>divided</u> between the rich <u>upper classes</u> (who owned the land) and the poorer <u>working classes</u>.
*   Throughout the 19th century, the <u>Industrial Revolution</u> was creating opportunities for more people to make more <u>money</u>.
*   This meant that the <u>middle classes</u> grew in <u>number</u> and <u>influence</u> throughout the century.

Education

*   In the <u>early</u> 19th century, <u>few</u> children went to school. Children from poor families often <u>worked</u> to help support their families instead.
*   In the <u>late</u> 19th century, <u>education reforms</u> made school <u>compulsory</u> for all young children.
*   <u>Rich</u> families often sent their children to <u>boarding school</u>, or hired a <u>governess</u> to live with the family and teach the children at <u>home</u>.

Women

*   After they got married, most women were expected to be in charge of looking after the <u>home</u> and <u>children</u>.
*   Women didn't have as many <u>rights</u> as men — they couldn't <u>vote</u> in elections and they often didn't <u>control</u> their own money and property.

Religion

*   Most <u>middle- and upper-class</u> people attended <u>church</u> regularly.
*   However, <u>science</u> was starting to challenge some religious ideas, e.g. Darwin's theory of <u>evolution</u> questioned the Bible's account of <u>creation</u>.

19th-Century Texts

Have a look at this piece of 19th-century writing

This is a letter written to Princess (later Queen) Victoria of the United Kingdom by her uncle, King Leopold I of Belgium. In it, Leopold describes his new wife, Louise Marie.

Laeken, 31st August 1832.

MY DEAREST LOVE,—You told me you wished to have a description of your new Aunt. I therefore shall both mentally and physically describe her to you.

She is extremely gentle and amiable, her actions are always guided by principles. She is at all times ready and disposed to sacrifice her comfort and inclinations to see others happy. She values goodness, merit, and virtue much more than beauty, riches, and amusements. With all this she is highly informed and very clever; she speaks and writes English, German and Italian; she speaks English very well indeed. In short, my dear Love, you see that I may well recommend her as an example for all young ladies, being Princesses or not.

Now to her appearance. She is about Feodore's* height, her hair very fair, light blue eyes, of a very gentle, intelligent and kind expression. A Bourbon** nose and small mouth. The figure is much like Feodore's but rather less stout. She rides very well, which she proved to my great alarm the other day, by keeping her seat though a horse of mine ran away with her full speed for at least half a mile. What she does particularly well is dancing. Music unfortunately she is not very fond of, though she plays on the harp; I believe there is some idleness in the case. There exists already great confidence and affection between us; she is desirous of doing everything that can contribute to my happiness, and I study whatever can make her happy and contented.

You will see by these descriptions that though my good little wife is not the tallest Queen, she is a very great prize which I highly value and cherish...

Now it is time I should finish my letter. Say everything that is kind to good Lehzen***, and believe me ever, my dearest Love, your faithful Friend and Uncle,

LEOPOLD R.

Glossary

* Feodore — Victoria's half-sister, Princess Feodora

** Bourbon — the Bourbons were the French royal family

*** Lehzen — Princess Victoria's governess, Louise Lehzen

Annotations:

The tone is affectionate but the register is formal — this is common in 19th-century letters.

Being 'virtuous' was an important quality in 19th-century society — it means having strong morals.

Upper-class women were considered to be accomplished by their ability in things like riding, dancing, playing music and speaking languages.

19th-century texts often phrase things differently — here, a modern writer might have said "I should end this letter here."

Upper-class women were educated in European languages in the 19th century.

This shows the 19th-century viewpoint of what was valued in upper-class women.

You might come across a tricky phrase or sentence. Use the context and the rest of the sentence to work out what's going on. Here, Leopold suggests that Louise Marie doesn't try very hard at playing the harp.

Women were often seen as belonging to their husbands.

Superlatives (e.g. 'kindest', 'most gracious') are common in 19th-century writing.

19th-century texts — unlikely to contain any emojis...

It's important to make sure you're comfortable reading and understanding 19th-century texts. This stuff might look a bit like History rather than English, but it'll really help you to improve some of your answers in the exam.

Tone

Tone can be a tricky little thing to put your finger on sometimes, but it comes through in the text's language.

Tone is the general feeling created by the text

1) A writer's tone is the <u>feeling</u> the words are written with, which creates a particular <u>mood</u> and shows the <u>attitude</u> of the writer. For example, the tone of a text might be:

- happy or sad
- serious or funny
- sombre or light-hearted
- emotional and passionate or cool and logical

Think of a writer's tone as being like someone's tone of voice when they're talking.

2) The main way to identify a text's tone is by looking at the <u>language</u>. For example, if a writer has used <u>informal</u> language, the tone might be quite <u>personal</u> or <u>familiar</u>, but <u>formal</u> language would suggest a more <u>serious</u> or <u>distant</u> tone.

3) <u>Punctuation</u> can also give you a clue about tone. For example, if there are lots of exclamation marks, that might suggest that the tone is very <u>emotional</u> or <u>passionate</u>.

4) Tone can reflect the <u>purpose</u> of a text (e.g. informative texts usually have a serious tone) or the <u>audience</u> (e.g. a playful tone might suggest a younger audience).

"You will not take that tone with me, good Sir Knight!"

Look closely at language to work out a text's tone

PAPER 1

A5. "In this passage, the writer makes the reader feel uneasy."
To what extent do you agree with this view?

> Phillipa stood on the cold, dark street, peering up at the abandoned hotel. Large wooden boards stood impassively across most of the window frames, sentries to the stillness and silence within, guarding the eerie presence of the dilapidated building.
>
> Despite her misgivings, she pushed gently on the front door, and it crept open with an arthritic creak. As she tiptoed over the threshold, small clouds of dust wheezed out of the carpet where she put her feet.

The adjectives used help to create the foreboding tone.

The sinister tone is gripping for the reader, which keeps the text entertaining.

Don't forget to mention how much you agree or disagree with the statement.

Remember to use technical terms wherever possible.

I strongly agree with this view. The heavily foreboding tone, created by adjectives such as "abandoned", "eerie" and "dilapidated", and reinforced by the personification of the "wooden boards" as silent "sentries", gives the passage a tense atmosphere. The reader shares in the fear and anxiety of the character, as you feel that something shocking could happen at any moment. The imagery of something cold and emotionless watching over the character makes you feel her vulnerability and fear for what might happen next.

Mention the combined effect of different features of the text.

You need to make sure you refer back to the statement for questions like this.

My mum always told me to watch my tone...

Sometimes, the tone will jump right out at you. But watch out for texts that are written with an ironic or sarcastic tone — the words might not mean exactly what they seem to at first (take a look at pages 33-34).

Style and Register

Every text you come across will be written in a particular style, using a particular register...

Style is how the text is written

1) A text's style is the overall way in which it's written, which includes language choices, sentence forms and structure.

2) There are lots of different styles you might encounter. E.g. cinematic, where the text is written as if the reader is watching a film, or journalistic which is a balanced way of writing reported news.

3) Register is the specific language (choice of words) used to match the writing to the social situation that it's for. Different situations require different registers, for example:

Register can be thought of as a part of style.

> If you wrote a letter to your local MP to ask them to stop the closure of a local leisure centre, you might use a formal register (e.g. 'the closure will have a detrimental effect'). This is because the audience is an authority figure that you don't know.

> If you wrote a letter to your friend to tell them about the leisure centre closure, you might use an informal register (e.g. 'it'll be rubbish when it shuts'). This is because the audience is someone you're familiar and friendly with.

4) Look out for how writers adapt their style and register to suit the purpose and the audience they are writing for.

Write about style and register when analysing language

A2. The author is trying to persuade the reader to try snowboarding. How does he try to do this?

Uses non-Standard English e.g. 'ain't'.

> I mean, come on, snowboarding is by far the coolest, craziest sport out there. Who's gonna argue with that? Here at SportFreakz magazine, we know what it's all about when it comes to extreme sports, and we can tell you that there ain't nothing else that gets the adrenaline pumping more than jumping on a board and flying down some snow-covered slopes.
>
> Ski season's upon us, guys. So book a flight, grab your board and get out to the Alps before all that snow melts! You just know you wanna!

The text is full of colloquial language, e.g. 'come on'.

The use of the second person makes it seem more personal.

Give examples to show what makes the register informal and youthful.

The text uses an informal, youthful register, with non-Standard English such as "ain't nothing else", and colloquial language like "come on", "gonna" and "wanna". These contribute to the text's conversational style, which is likely to appeal to a younger audience because it mirrors the way they might speak. This could persuade a younger reader by helping them to identify with the writer, so that they are more likely to want to try an activity that the writer recommends.

Discuss how the style creates the desired effect on the reader.

Develop your point with the overall effect of the text.

Yep, if there's one thing I know, it's style...

Style has to do with lots of things — language and vocabulary, structure, tone... so just think about how the style is built up from all these different bits and you'll be laughing in the exam. Well, not too loud, mind...

Words and Phrases

Writers don't just chuck in any old words — they painstakingly select them to produce the desired effect...

Writers use a range of word types

It's important to be able to identify the types of words that a writer is using.
Have a look at the definitions below to remind you:

> Nouns are naming words — they might refer to a person, place, thing or idea, e.g. sister, pen, art.
>
> A pronoun is a word that replaces a noun, e.g. he, she, it, them.
>
> Possessive pronouns are pronouns that show ownership, e.g. his, hers, ours, theirs.
>
> Verbs are action words, e.g. think, run, swim, shout.
>
> Adjectives describe a noun or pronoun, e.g. happy, clever, interesting.
>
> Adverbs give extra information about verbs, e.g. quickly, loudly, accidentally.

Words and phrases can be used to achieve different effects

1) For the reading questions (Section A on both papers), you need to pay close attention to the reasons why a writer has used particular words or phrases.

2) Words can have subtle implications beyond their obvious meaning — these are called 'connotations'. For example:

Analysing the connotations of words is a way of 'reading with insight'. There's more on this on pages 8-9.

Pedro shut the door. *Pedro slammed the door.*	When the verb 'shut' is used, it doesn't imply anything about Pedro's emotions. The verb 'slammed' has a similar meaning to 'shut', but it gives the impression that Pedro is angry or tense.
I sniggered when I saw Peter's costume. *I chuckled when I saw Peter's costume.*	The verbs 'sniggered' and 'chuckled' both mean the writer laughed, but 'sniggered' has a slightly nastier connotation — as if the writer is making fun of Peter.

3) Words are often chosen to achieve particular effects. For example:

my dear reader *your beloved pet*	Phrases that use the possessive determiners 'my', 'your' and 'our' help to establish familiarity between the writer and the reader.

Determiners are words that help to identify nouns — in this case, they show who the noun belongs to.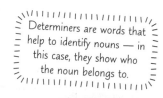

a fundamentally flawed proposition *a totally unbelievable situation*	Some phrases use intensifiers to make the text seem more emotive and powerful. Intensifiers are adverbs like 'very', 'really' or 'extremely' that are used alongside strong adjectives to provide emphasis.

Words and Phrases

Words work together to create cumulative effects

1) Writers can use the words from a specific <u>semantic field</u> (the words associated with a particular <u>theme</u> or <u>topic</u>) to convey an idea to the reader. For example:

> *Dessert was simply <u>divine</u>; a <u>cloud-like</u> puff of pastry that was lighter than an <u>angel's wing</u>.*

> Here, the <u>semantic field</u> of <u>heaven</u> is used to make something sound <u>appealing</u>.

2) Keep an eye out for situations where particular <u>types</u> of words are <u>repeated</u>, e.g. sentences with lots of <u>adjectives</u> or paragraphs with lots of <u>verbs</u>.

3) You could comment on the <u>cumulative effect</u> of particular types of words — show you've thought about how the words in the text <u>work together</u> to create <u>tone</u> or <u>affect</u> the reader in some way, e.g.

> *Adjectives like 'electrifying', 'thrilling', 'tense' and 'intriguing' create a cumulative effect of <u>excitement</u>.*

> *The adverbs 'jovially', 'readily' and 'pleasantly' combine to create an impression of <u>enjoyment</u>.*

> Archie was keen to understand the cumulative effect of the words.

© Fly_dragonfly/iStockphoto.com

Try to pick out significant words and phrases

PAPER 2

A2. The author is trying to persuade us to choose Bijoux Birthdays. How do they try to do this?

> Adjectives like 'magical', 'beautiful', 'balmy', 'glistening' and 'sumptuous' have a pleasant cumulative effect — they create a calming atmosphere.

> Watch out for repeated grammatical constructions — they give the text emphasis.

> Imperatives like 'sit back' and 'let us' give the text an authoritative tone, whilst the words 'perhaps' and 'maybe' give the impression that the reader has a choice.

A PICTURE-PERFECT PICNIC

Bijoux Birthdays invite you to celebrate your special day in style. Join us for a magical evening of entertainment on the beautiful banks of the River Fairer. Let us help you to relax in the balmy atmosphere of a warm summer's evening, recline next to the glistening waters and indulge in the most sumptuous of picnics.

We can tailor your evening to suit you. We can provide a refreshing feast for your senses. We can transport you to another place and time. Just sit back and let us do all the work. All you need to do is relax.

We have a large selection of menus for you to choose from, as well as a whole host of different entertainment acts — maybe you'd like a string quartet, or perhaps you'd be more interested in a circus act? Whatever your tastes, rest assured that we will be able to accommodate you.

> Phrases that use possessive determiners establish familiarity with the reader and make the text more persuasive.

> The list of three verbs — 'relax', 'recline' and 'indulge' — gives the text a convincing tone and makes the offer sound inviting.

Relax, it's just a phrase...

The technical grammar of words and phrases is important, but it's no good just pointing it out — you need to analyse its effects. Think about why certain words and phrases have been used and the impression they create.

Metaphors and Similes

Metaphors and similes are both types of imagery — writers use them to help readers imagine things vividly.

Metaphors and similes are comparisons

1) Metaphors and similes describe one thing by <u>comparing</u> it to something else.

| <u>Metaphors</u> describe something by saying that it <u>is</u> something else. | → | *His gaze <u>was</u> a laser beam, shooting straight through me.* |

| <u>Similes</u> describe something by saying that it's <u>like</u> something else. They usually use the words <u>as</u> or <u>like</u>. | → | *Walking through the bog was <u>like</u> wading through treacle.* |

Similes made Jeremy feel as if the world had been turned upside down.

2) They help writers to make their <u>descriptions</u> more creative and interesting.

3) Metaphors usually create a <u>more powerful image</u> than similes, because they describe something as if it <u>actually were</u> something else.

See pages 21-22 for more on literature and literary non-fiction.

4) Metaphors and similes are most commonly used in <u>literature</u> and <u>literary non-fiction</u>.

Comment on the effect of metaphors and similes

PAPER 1

A2. How does the writer show what life as a soldier is like?

Uses 'like' so it's a simile. →

The air clung to me like a warm, wet blanket. It was like living inside a horribly stifling nightmare. I just wanted to wake up, throw the blanket off the bed and breathe some cool, fresh air.

After a while, I couldn't tell what was nightmare and what wasn't. Once I was caught in an ambush, taking fire from three sides. The order came to fall back, and I found myself on my own. I tried to run, but my feet were blocks of concrete. ←

It's a metaphor, as he says his feet actually 'were' blocks of concrete.

Make sure you use technical terms.

Remember the question — keep referring back to how language has been used to describe the soldier's life.

The writer uses a simile to describe what the conditions felt like: "The air clung to me like a warm, wet blanket". This image really helps the reader to imagine how unpleasant and sticky it feels, but also helps to create a hostile and suffocating atmosphere.

By using the metaphor "my feet were blocks of concrete", the writer suggests a feeling of extreme heaviness in the soldier's feet, which conveys his panic that, try as he might, he was too scared to flee. The use of these images makes the description effective because it helps the reader to empathise with the soldier.

Develop your points by stating the effect of the language.

I met a phor once — he was a number...

Picking out imagery, such as metaphors and similes, will help you to closely analyse the language used in the exam texts. Remember to comment on the <u>effect</u> that the writer's choice of language has, though.

Analogy

Analogies are nifty little tricks which writers often use when they're writing to argue or persuade.

Analogies are really fancy comparisons

1) An analogy <u>compares</u> one idea to another to make it easier to <u>understand</u>.

2) Analogies provide <u>powerful</u> and <u>memorable</u> images. They can be more <u>familiar</u> or more <u>shocking</u> than the original idea, which makes it easier for the reader to <u>grasp the point</u>. For example:

> *Deforestation is happening at an incredible speed. An area of rainforest equal to twenty football pitches is lost every minute.* → By <u>comparing</u> the area to football pitches, the writer makes it easier to <u>visualise</u> the scale of the problem.

> *Hoping your exams will go OK without opening your books is like hoping to win the lottery without buying a ticket.* → By <u>comparing</u> the chances of success to an impossible situation, the writer <u>emphasises</u> that it is very unlikely.

Analogies are like extended similes (see p.29) — they also often use the word 'like'.

3) Analogies are common in <u>non-fiction</u> texts that are trying to <u>argue</u> a point or <u>persuade</u>, as they can help to get the writer's viewpoint across <u>clearly</u> and <u>forcefully</u>.

Think about why the writer has used an analogy

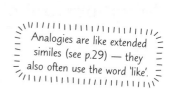

A2. The author is trying to persuade the reader to reduce their emissions. How does she try to do this?

> It's easy to throw facts and figures around, but very few people realise we are releasing almost 30 billion tonnes of greenhouse gases into the atmosphere every year. That's the equivalent of around 150 million blue whales.
>
> By pumping these gases into the air, we are choking our planet. This is like starting a fire in your bedroom and slowly letting the room fill with thick, black smoke until you can't breathe.

Uses 'like', so this is another analogy.

The word 'equivalent' shows that this is a comparison.

It's good to make your point straight away.

The writer uses analogies to help persuade the reader. By comparing the amount of greenhouse gases released annually to "150 million blue whales", the writer helps the reader to understand and visualise the sheer volume of gas being produced. If they can visualise the problem, readers are more likely to be shocked and therefore share the writer's concerns.

It's great to embed quotes into your writing like this.

The analogy which compares polluting the atmosphere to filling your bedroom with "thick, black smoke" makes the threat of climate change seem like a more personal danger to the reader. This might scare the reader and help to persuade them to act on climate change.

Always mention the effect that language has on the reader.

I think I may have developed analogy to this page...

Writers use analogies to make their points clearer and easier to understand. They can also make a piece of writing more interesting — think about how you could use them in the writing section of your exams.

Section Three — Reading: Language and Structure

Personification

If it's info on personification you're after, sit back and let this page talk you through it...

Personification is describing a thing as a person

1) Personification describes something as if it's a <u>person</u>. This could be in the way something <u>looks</u>, <u>moves</u>, <u>sounds</u> or some other aspect of it. For example:

Describing an object as if it were alive

The desk groaned under the weight of the books.

Describing an abstract idea as if it were alive

Fear stalked the children with every step they took.

Describing an animal as if it were a person

The cunning fox smiled with a self-satisfied grin.

Try to think of other ways you could use personification in your own writing.

2) Personification makes a description <u>more vivid</u> (so it '<u>comes to life</u>' for the reader).

3) It can also help to give a sense of the <u>viewpoint</u> or <u>attitude</u> of the <u>writer</u> or <u>character</u>:

Military helicopters prowled the city, their menacing mechanical voices threatening to stamp out the smallest sign of activity. → This shows that the writer feels that the helicopters are an <u>intimidating</u> presence.

Think about the effect of personification

PAPER 1

A4. How does the writer make these lines calm and positive?

> To Catrin's mind, no pastime could better complement a summer's day than a stroll through the woodlands behind her uncle's house.
>
> As soon as she arrived, before she'd even unpacked, she would feel the forest calling to her. It was never long before she wandered into the cool embrace of the sunlight-dappled shade. The trees would smile as she meandered along the paths, and the friendly chatter of wildlife was always the very best company.

The forest has been given human qualities.

The shade has been personified as it embraces the girl.

The writer uses personification to create a calm, positive atmosphere in the story. The smiling trees and the "friendly chatter of wildlife" present parts of the forest as if they were friends of Catrin, which shows that she feels relaxed and at home around them. This is reinforced further by how she is embraced by the "sunlight-dappled shade". By presenting Catrin and the woods as old friends, the writer keeps the reader feeling calm and positive about what is happening to Catrin as the story progresses.

This is a paraphrase — mentioning something from the text without a direct quote.

Examiners love short embedded quotes like this one.

This is good — it explains the effect of the language.

Link your points back to the question, and mention how the text affects the reader.

The exam papers cackled as the students filed in...

So personification's a bit of a tricky customer — it's not always as simple to spot as you'd think. When you're writing about personification, concentrate on why the writer's used it and what effect it has on the reader.

Alliteration and Onomatopoeia

Here's heaps hof hinformation hall habout halliteration hand honomatopoeia. Wait a minute...

Alliteration and onomatopoeia are about how words sound

1) Alliteration and onomatopoeia use the <u>sounds</u> of words to create an <u>effect</u>:

<u>Alliteration</u> is when words that are close together begin with the <u>same sound</u>.
→ *PM's panic!*
Close call for kids

<u>Onomatopoeic</u> words <u>sound like</u> the noises they describe.
→ *thud   crackle   squish   hiss   smash*

Naina was less than impressed with Chris's attempt to spell 'onomatopoeia'.

2) <u>Alliteration</u> helps a writer to grab a reader's <u>attention</u>.

3) It's often used for <u>emphasis</u> and to make key points more <u>memorable</u>.

4) <u>Onomatopoeia</u> makes descriptions more <u>powerful</u> — it appeals to the reader's sense of <u>hearing</u>, which helps them <u>imagine</u> what the writer is describing.

Alliteration and onomatopoeia keep readers interested

PAPER 2

A2. The author is trying to persuade the reader to buy Milkshake Magic. How does he try to do this?

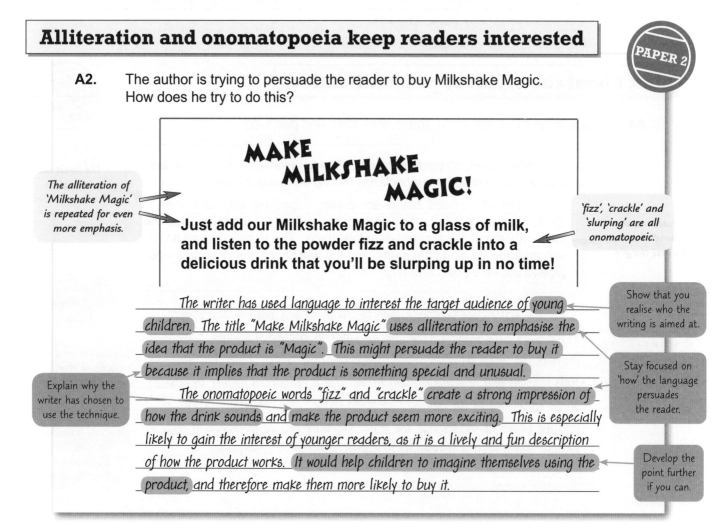

Wait — how many vowels? No, that can't be right...

Yep, the first challenge that this page presents is learning to spell 'onomatopoeia'... But once you've got your head around that, you can enjoy the bloomin' brilliant bang that this page can bring to your writing.

Section Three — Reading: Language and Structure

Irony

Irony — nothing to do with clothes or metal, everything to do with the tone of a piece of writing.

Irony is saying the opposite of what you mean

1) Irony is when the <u>literal meaning</u> of a piece of writing is the exact <u>opposite</u> of its <u>intended meaning</u>.

2) The reader can tell the writer is being ironic from the <u>context</u> of the writing.

3) Writers often use irony to express their viewpoint, but it helps to make what they're saying more <u>humorous</u> or <u>light-hearted</u>.

It was pouring down with rain — perfect weather for a barbecue. → The <u>context</u> (the rainy weather) shows that the writer actually means that it was <u>terrible</u> weather for a barbecue.

Irony can sometimes be a little tricky to spot

A5. "In this passage, the writer makes the character's feelings really clear. It feels as if you really get to know her."

To what extent do you agree with this view?

Clara sat on her lounger at the edge of the pool, thinking of all the poor souls still trapped in the office. She'd been asked to travel to Spain for work. Stay hunched over her cramped, stuffy desk in London or work in this paradise? A very difficult decision indeed.

As the sun rose higher in the sky and the temperature crept up, she thought of dreary, cloudy London. "It's a tough job" she thought to herself, "but somebody's got to do it".

You can tell she is being ironic because of the context — she describes it as a 'paradise', so it can't have been a 'difficult decision'.

I agree with the first part of this statement, though Clara's feelings are potentially open to misinterpretation. Her comments about a "difficult decision" and a "tough job" are negative if read literally, but the context makes it clear that they should be taken ironically. She clearly prefers being in Spain. Her office in London is "cramped", and the people are "trapped", whereas Spain is a "paradise". The irony emphasises just how happy she is by highlighting this contrast.

I also strongly agree with the second part of the statement. Her ironic tone shows that she isn't too serious, but that she is also perhaps quite unsympathetic. The contrast between her situation and that of the "poor souls" in the London office shows that whilst she is "thinking of all" of them, she is most interested in her own pleasant situation. As a reader, this makes me unsure as to whether I like her character or not.

Don't forget to mention how much you agree or disagree with the statement.

Make sure you clearly explain why the language is ironic.

A further personal response is a good way to develop your answer.

Irony, yeah right, what a great technique...

It might seem confusing that exactly the same words can mean completely opposite things, but the context usually makes it fairly clear when a writer is trying to be ironic — otherwise it wouldn't be very effective.

Sarcasm

The word 'sarcasm' comes from a Greek word that means 'flesh tearing', so you just know it's gonna be fun.

Sarcasm is nastier than irony

1) Sarcasm is language that has a mocking or scornful tone. It's often intended to insult someone or make fun of them, or to show that the writer is angry or annoyed about something.

2) Sarcastic writing usually uses irony — but the tone is more aggressive and unpleasant.

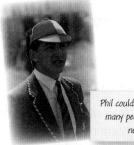

Phil couldn't believe how many people liked his new hat.

> The food took 90 minutes to arrive, which was just brilliant. I can think of no better way to spend a Saturday evening than waiting around for a plate of mediocre mush.

The writer's used irony and a sarcastic tone to show his frustration and anger — it's meant to insult the restaurant that kept him waiting.

3) Satire is a kind of writing that uses sarcasm to make fun of a particular person or thing — it's often used in journalism and reviews.

Explain how you can tell a comment is sarcastic

PAPER 2

A6. Both of these texts are about an economic proposal. Compare the following:
- the writers' attitudes to the proposal;
- how they get across their arguments.

Source A

The Government's new economic proposal lays out an excellent path for our economy. Their plan will put more money where it is needed, which is exactly what this country needs right now.

This shows a clearly positive attitude...

... so this feels like a sincere opinion.

Source B

The Government's really outdone itself with this latest economic plan. A lovely gift to the taxpayers, who will now be under even greater financial strain. All in all, exactly what this country needs right now.

The context is negative...

... so this feels like a sarcastic tone.

Nice opening — it gets straight to the point.

The writers' opinions differ greatly. Source A looks at the Government's new plan as a positive thing, describing it as "excellent", whereas Source B uses a heavily sarcastic tone to criticise it. The plan is clearly not a "lovely gift to the taxpayers", as they will be under more "financial strain".

It is interesting that both writers describe the economic proposal as "exactly" what the country "needs", but with different effects. Source A's tone is sincere, whereas the negative context of Source B makes it clear that the writer is being sarcastic, and believes that the plan is in fact the exact opposite of "what this country needs right now". This method of ridiculing the Government's plan may influence the reader to agree with the writer's point of view by making the proposal seem so ridiculous that it can't be taken seriously.

Use short quotes within your own sentences.

Use technical terms.

Explain how you know that the writer's being sarcastic.

Explain the effect on the reader.

Explain the effect that the use of sarcasm has.

Oh great, now sarcasm — even better than irony...

So the Greeks may have been on to something with the whole 'flesh tearing' thing... Sarcasm is often used to ridicule someone or something. Not the nicest thing to do, perhaps, but you can't say it's not effective.

Section Three — Reading: Language and Structure

Rhetoric

Rhetorical techniques make language more persuasive — see if this page can persuade you to keep going...

There are lots of rhetorical techniques

Think about how other techniques (e.g. alliteration, sarcasm) could be used as rhetorical devices.

1) Rhetorical questions require no answer — they make readers engage with the text and realise the answer for themselves. This makes the reader feel like they're making up their own mind, when actually the writer is trying to make them think a certain way.

> Is it right that footballers are paid such vast sums of money?

2) Writers often use a list of three words or phrases to emphasise the point they're making. They often use three adjectives.

> The cross-country run is painful, pointless and pure evil.

3) Hyperbole is intentional exaggeration. It's used to make a point very powerfully.

> We had to wait forever for the food to arrive.

4) Antithesis is a technique where opposing words or ideas are presented together to show a contrast.

> Just a small donation from you could have huge consequences for others.

5) Parenthesis is when an extra clause or phrase is inserted into a complete sentence. Parenthesis can be used in many ways, such as to add extra information or to directly address the reader.

> This issue, as I'm sure you all agree, is of the highest importance.

Rhetorical devices add impact to an argument

PAPER 2

A2. The author is trying to persuade the reader that students shouldn't be given more homework. How does he try to do this?

> This plan to give students across the country more homework is shocking. Can it really be fair to set us even more ridiculous and unnecessary assignments? It's as if they don't think we work every hour God sends already! Join me if you're interested in a better work/life balance. Join me to make our voices heard. Join me in my campaign for less homework!

This is a rhetorical question.

The writer repeats 'join me' three times.

Here's some hyperbole.

The writer uses 'we' and 'us' to include the reader.

The writer uses a number of rhetorical devices to persuade the reader that students should not be given more homework. The rhetorical question about whether it's fair to set more homework assignments is used to engage the reader. When combined with the forceful adjectives "ridiculous" and "unnecessary", this makes the reader think that it isn't fair, and therefore agree with the writer's point of view. This is immediately followed by the assertion that students are already working "every hour God sends". This hyperbolic statement makes an emphatic point about how hard students work, which generates sympathy from the reader and enhances the argument that more homework would be "shocking".

Analysing the effect on the reader develops 'how' the writer has argued their point.

It's good to link your points together wherever possible.

Opening statement is really focused on 'how' the writer argues their point.

Using the writer's words really backs up your analysis of their viewpoint.

Revision is a fun, exciting, thrilling way to spend a Friday night...

Rhetoric is a powerful tool, but I'm not sure it can convince us to love revision... Remember, there are lots of different types of rhetorical techniques, so keep your eyes peeled. Peeled eyes — now that's disgusting...

Bias

If a text is biased, it doesn't give a balanced view — the writer's opinion affects the writing.

Biased writing is affected by the writer's opinions

1) Biased writers don't usually lie, but they don't give a <u>balanced overview</u> of an argument.

2) Sometimes the writer <u>won't mention</u> something that opposes their viewpoint, or they'll <u>exaggerate</u> something that supports it.

3) Biased writing also often uses <u>generalisations</u> — sweeping statements that aren't necessarily true.

4) Bias isn't always <u>obvious</u>, or even <u>deliberate</u>. Biased writers often <u>seem</u> to be talking in a neutral, factual way — while actually only presenting one point of view.

5) You need to be able to <u>recognise</u> bias, so that you don't mistake opinion for fact.

6) Look out for bias in non-fiction texts like <u>newspaper articles</u> and <u>reviews</u>.

Sylvester's essay on who was boss wasn't the slightest bit biased.

Bias weakens a writer's argument

PAPER 2

A6. Both of these texts are about *Romeo and Juliet*. Compare the following:
* the writers' attitudes to *Romeo and Juliet*;
* how they get across their arguments.

19th-century review

Romeo and Juliet, without the slightest shadow of a doubt, is the very greatest work of literature to have ever been penned in the English language.
It truly is the pinnacle of Shakespeare's momentous talent and will never be matched by any playwright to come.

Biased writers may use hyperbole if they are trying to convince you about something.

They often make opinions sound like facts.

21st-century biography

Romeo and Juliet is one of the most well-known and widely studied works of literature to have ever been penned in the English language.
It was among the most popular of Shakespeare's plays during his lifetime, and it is still performed to this day.

The review is written in a very biased way. Hyperbolic statements such as "without the slightest shadow of a doubt" emphasise the writer's strength of feeling, but the statements are unjustified. This bias presents the reader with an emphatic argument for how good the play is, but nothing to back it up. This may convince some readers to watch the play, but others may feel the argument is quite weak.
    Although the biography is also positive about 'Romeo and Juliet', the writer bases their viewpoint on factual statements, describing the play as "well-known" and "widely studied". The writer of the biography is also careful to use phrases like "one of the most" and "among the most", which shows that they are aware that there are other successful and popular plays. Overall, the biography presents a more balanced viewpoint towards Romeo and Juliet.

Develop your point by writing about the writer's purpose and how successful they are.

Try to use more interesting vocabulary to get across your exact meaning.

Mention the overall difference between the two texts.

We're too expensive for you — you'll never bias...

A good way to spot bias is when the writer presents their opinion as fact (by saying something confidently), but giving no evidence for it. This weakens their argument, as you can claim all sorts of absurd things this way.

Section Three — Reading: Language and Structure

Descriptive Language

Descriptive language pops its head up all over the place — writers just love it. Better get stuck in, then...

Descriptive language makes text interesting

1) Writers use descriptive <u>techniques</u> and <u>vocabulary</u> so that the reader gets a really clear <u>image</u> in their mind of what the writer's describing. It makes the text more <u>interesting</u>, <u>dramatic</u> and <u>convincing</u>.

2) <u>Descriptive techniques</u> include <u>imagery</u> such as metaphors, similes and personification (see p.29-31).

3) Writers often give <u>descriptions</u> based on their five <u>senses</u> (what they can <u>see</u>, <u>smell</u>, <u>hear</u>, <u>touch</u> or <u>taste</u>).

4) Another sign of descriptive language is when the writer uses lots of <u>adjectives</u> — describing words like 'huge' or 'fiery' that give a specific <u>impression</u> of something.

5) Writers might also use interesting <u>verbs</u>, such as 'saunter' instead of 'walk' to make their descriptions really <u>specific</u>.

The sun was setting over the sea. The view from the beach was incredible.	This example relies on the reader to picture <u>for themselves</u> what a nice sunset might look like.
The salty sea air whooshed around me as the dark-orange sun melted into the horizon, dyeing the cobalt sky a deep crimson.	This one uses interesting <u>adjectives</u> and <u>verbs</u> to help the reader to picture and even 'feel' what's going on.

6) Writers can also <u>build up</u> the description of something <u>throughout</u> their work. For example, by writing sentences with <u>contrasting</u> descriptions or descriptions that <u>agree</u> with each other.

Talk about the effects of specific words

PAPER 1

A3. What impressions do you get about how Henry feels from these lines?

Describes the smell to add to the description.

Uses a lot of interesting verbs and adjectives.

Henry crept slowly towards the tall, dark, brooding building, coming to a standstill in its looming shadow. Smoke billowed from its many chimneys, stinging his eyes and filling his nostrils with an overpowering, acrid smell. He watched the other workers scuttling in through the iron gates. With the tall building glowering down at him, he shuddered, forced his right foot out in front of his left, and began to traipse towards the doors.

The building is personified to emphasise that it is intimidating.

The writer uses descriptive language to make it clear that Henry is feeling very intimidated. The verbs "crept" and "traipse" both carry a negative connotation: they imply walking very slowly and reluctantly, as if the character is unwilling to approach the building. His reluctance is also shown in the phrase, "forced his right foot out in front of his left". The verb "forced", coupled with the extra detail of exactly how he moved his feet, shows that it is a considerable effort.

It's great to talk about the effects of specific words.

Mention if language techniques work together to create an effect.

My dad used descriptive language when I scratched his car...

Descriptive language comes in all shapes and sizes. Look out for it in the literature text in paper 1, and in any literary non-fiction you get in paper 2. Be prepared to write about the effect descriptive language has...

Narrative Viewpoint

Literature will always have a narrator — a voice that is telling the story.

The narrative viewpoint is usually quite easy to spot

1) A <u>first-person narrator</u> tells the story using words like 'I', 'we' and 'me'. A first-person narrator is often one of the <u>characters</u>, telling the reader <u>directly</u> about their feelings and experiences.

> *I stood on the fringes of the stage, waiting my turn, fear coursing through my veins.* → A first-person narrator establishes a <u>stronger</u>, more <u>personal</u> connection with the reader.

2) A <u>second-person narrator</u> tells the story using words like 'you'. A second-person narrator talks as if the reader ('you') <u>is</u> one of the characters.

> *You turn your head to see her walking towards you. Your heart begins to race.* → A second-person narrator makes the reader '<u>feel</u>' what the character is feeling.

3) A <u>third-person narrator</u> is not one of the characters. They tell the story using words like 'he' and 'she' to talk <u>about</u> the characters.

> *Ian's elated expression could mean only one thing: he had got a place at medical school.* → A third-person narrator has a more <u>detached</u> viewpoint.

Some third-person narrators are omniscient — they know what all the characters are thinking. Others are limited — they only know what one character is thinking.

4) When writing about a narrator, think about how <u>reliable</u> they are. You might not be able to <u>trust</u> them fully if they <u>don't know something</u>, or if they're trying to <u>affect</u> the reader in some way.

Think about how the narrator presents the characters

A5. "In this passage, the writer presents Alice as an annoying character."

To what extent do you agree with this view?

Uses 'she' and is separate to the characters, so it's a third-person narrator.

> Polly was walking down the corridor when she noticed that Alice was walking towards her. Polly sighed, rolled her eyes and braced herself.
> "Hi Polly!" chirped Alice, with her typically exhausting optimism, "I hope I'll see you at the party later!"
> Polly's face contorted into an obviously forced smile as she nodded sharply.

Think carefully about how the narrator's perspective is being used to affect the reader.

> I strongly agree with the evaluation. The writer has used the narrator's perspective to present Alice as annoying, despite her actions. Everything she does is positive: she is bright, friendly, optimistic and simply invites Polly to a party. The narrator presents her optimism as "typically exhausting" though, so her actions come across to the reader as tiresome, rather than positive. This is reinforced by the narrator's heavy focus on Polly's expressions, which all betray her personal dislike for Alice: she "rolled" her eyes and had a "forced smile".

Link your points together to give a really detailed analysis of what the writer has done.

Narrator race — 'I' was first, 'you' were second, 'he' was third...

It can be quite easy to forget about the narrator, because they're often not one of the characters directly involved in the story. But try to think about how they talk, and also if you can trust what they tell you.

Structure — Non-Fiction Texts

Structure is the way a writer organises their ideas within a text. On this page, there's some information about how non-fiction texts use structure — turn over to find out more about structure in fiction texts.

Structure can help to achieve the writer's purpose

Writing to Argue or Persuade

- When writing to argue or persuade, a writer may organise their points to gradually build up to a powerful conclusion. E.g. they might start with statistics, then build up to more emotive points.

- A writer might also use a counter-argument, where they will introduce the opposite viewpoint to their own, then explain why they disagree with it in order to build support for their own argument.

- They could also repeat specific words, sentences or ideas in order to emphasise important points.

Writing to Inform or Advise

- When writing to inform or advise, a writer will use a logical structure so that the information is clear and the reader can easily follow their advice.

- They could break up information so that it's less intimidating for the reader by using lots of paragraphs or numbered points.

- They could also include an introduction and a conclusion, to make their advice clear.

Think about how the text has been organised

PAPER 2

A2. How does the writer of this speech persuade the reader to eat more healthily?

This single-word paragraph helps to persuade the reader by emphasising the strength of the writer's emotions.

This paragraph introduces a new idea — a solution to the problems presented.

The first and last paragraphs start in the same way. This encourages the reader to think about how their opinion has changed.

> As a nation, we have a problem. A recent survey has revealed that a mere 30% of people regularly eat the full five portions of fruit and vegetables that our bodies require daily; a shocking 25% said that they didn't eat any fruit and vegetables at all on a day-to-day basis. Outrageous.
>
> How have we let this happen? It is simply astonishing that we've fallen into such bad eating habits; simply unforgiveable that we're teaching our children to rely on junk food and sugary rubbish instead of loading them up with the nutrients they require.
>
> It's time to make a change. I'm encouraging everybody to make a tiny tweak to their daily routine. You can make the decision to drop unhealthy, sugar-laden snacks in favour of a juicy apple or crunchy celery stick. You can make a difference to your health, and set a good example to the people around you.
>
> As a nation, perhaps we've gone a little astray, but I don't think it's too late to change our ways. If we work together, we can kick sugary snacks out of our lives, and embrace healthy living for a better future.

The text starts with facts and statistics to establish an authoritative tone and gain the reader's trust, then goes on to explain the author's opinions.

Repetition is used in these paragraphs to emphasise the writer's point of view and make the speech more memorable for the reader.

This book is structured so that you ace your exams...

Structure plays a huge part in every text you read, so you'll need to really get to grips with how it works. Think about the way the writer organises their ideas, and the order in which they're presented to the reader.

Structure — Fiction Texts

Now that you've got to grips with the structure of non-fiction texts, have a look at these two pages —
they're all about how writers use structure in fiction texts, like the one you'll get in paper 1, section A.

Fiction texts use structure to entertain their audience

1) In <u>fiction</u> texts, writers will structure their work in a way they think will <u>entertain</u> the reader. For example:

- Texts with a <u>linear</u> structure are arranged <u>chronologically</u> — events are described in the order in which they happened, and the text <u>flows</u> naturally from <u>beginning</u> to <u>middle</u> to <u>end</u>. They will often engage the reader's interest by <u>building</u> towards some form of <u>climax</u>.

- Texts with a <u>non-linear</u> structure are ordered in a way that makes the text <u>interesting</u>, rather than in chronological order. They might include things like <u>flashbacks</u>, changes in <u>perspective</u> (using different narrators) or <u>time shifts</u>.

2) Whenever you write about structure, you need to show <u>how</u> the writer has used structure to produce a particular effect on the <u>reader</u>.

Writers use structure to focus the reader's attention

One of the easiest ways to write about <u>structure</u> is to think about how the writer is <u>directing</u> your <u>attention</u> as you read. There are lots of ways a writer can do this, for example:

- The writer might draw the reader in by <u>describing</u> something <u>general</u>, then <u>narrow</u> their <u>focus</u> down to something more <u>specific</u>.

- The writer could <u>describe</u> things along a <u>journey</u> and make you feel as if you are travelling with them. This might involve moving from the <u>outside</u> to the <u>inside</u> or just from one place to another.

- A text might start with <u>description</u> and then move on to <u>dialogue</u>. This would shift your focus from <u>setting</u> to <u>characters</u>.

- Often, a writer will use a <u>new paragraph</u> to start a <u>new topic</u>. This could be a <u>smooth</u> transition, or it could have a <u>jarring</u> effect that draws the reader's attention to a particular part of the text.

The narrative viewpoint will affect the structure

1) The <u>narrator</u> controls what the reader <u>sees</u> and what <u>information</u> they <u>receive</u>, so different <u>narrators</u> will have different <u>effects</u> on the <u>structure</u> of a text:

"When you're a grown-up narrator, you can skip about too."

- A <u>third-person</u> narrator (see p.38) will often have an <u>overall</u> view of the story, so the structure might <u>skip around</u> to cover lots of <u>different</u> events.

- For texts with a <u>first-person</u> narrator, the structure will probably <u>follow</u> that character's experiences quite <u>closely</u>.

2) A narrator might also <u>withhold</u> some information to create <u>tension</u>, or they could <u>skip</u> over certain parts of a story because they are <u>biased</u>.

3) Look out for texts that have <u>more than one</u> narrator. This might mean that the structure <u>jumps around</u> or alternates between the different <u>perspectives</u>.

Structure — Fiction Texts

Think about what the writer wants the reader to focus on

PAPER 1

A4. How does the writer make these lines interesting for the reader?

The extract begins by focusing the reader's attention on the setting.

The mountain looked a little mysterious in the half-light of the dusky evening. Its snow-capped peak stood alert, bathing in the dying embers of the setting sun. From there, my eye was drawn to the narrow path that wound its way precariously down past the dark woods and craggy outcrops of the mountain face. I traced the weaving path all the way down, until it vanished behind the spire of a magnificent church that loomed over the town nestled at the foot of the mountain.

The 'narrow path' is used as a device to lead the reader's focus to the town below the mountains.

The one-line paragraph grabs the reader's attention by providing a contrast to the long descriptive paragraph before it.

This was the town of my youth.

This was the town where I had taken my first steps. This was the town where I had been to school, where I had battled through those tough transition years of teenage angst and, finally, where I had first fallen in love. It was permeated with memories of childhood games and, later in my adolescence, secret late-night trysts.

This time-shift switches the reader's attention from the setting to the narrator's childhood, which allows the reader to learn more about the character and her story.

I crossed the road and entered the alley that would take me deeper into the warren of streets that wound their way around the foot of the imposing church. When I finally emerged into the square, I was assaulted by a barrage of sights and smells that instantly took me all the way back to my youth.

The final sentence leads into the next paragraph so that the time-shift doesn't jar too much, and enables the reader to follow the action easily.

Immediately, I was back under the oak tree, crouching silently next to my best friend Sally. We were hiding from James Cotton, and it was a matter of grave honour that we preserved our hiding place.

This text has a non-linear structure — it skips forwards and backwards in time.

Back then, a game of hide and seek was no mere playground triviality. It was a fierce battle between the sexes, a passionately fought war between two equally resolute forces. We spent endless days squirrelled away in the nooks and crannies of the town we knew like the back of our hand, listening out warily for the tell-tale scramble of footsteps that meant James had found our hiding place.

This long sentence emphasises the 'endless days' of the narrator's childhood.

Paragraphs are used here to help the reader follow both the narrator's thoughts and her journey. They show changes in topic, time, character or place.

Both Sally and I were fascinated with James: he was old for his age, smart and funny. Obviously, at that age, this fascination manifested itself as bitter hatred. For me, the coyness would come later, at around the same time as the feelings of claustrophobia and a strong yearning for the big city. Sally hadn't felt the same longing for the metropolis as I had, but she had discovered the coyness that would replace the naive and innocent feud. She had stayed here and built a life for herself.

Tomorrow morning I was to attend the wedding at which she would become Mrs Cotton.

This single-sentence paragraph suggests that the wedding is going to be an important event in the story.

The structure of the text takes the reader along with the narrator on her journey through the town. The writer also uses this journey to take the reader on a second journey through the narrator's childhood.

The tolling of the church bells brought me back to the present with a start. I needed to hurry if I was to get to my parents' house before dinnertime. With a sigh of nostalgia, I turned away from the old oak tree, and began the final leg of the journey back to my former home...

Revision. Exam. Relaxation. — an example of a linear structure...

It can be tricky to think of something insightful to say about linear texts, because there aren't any snazzy time-shifts or flashbacks. If you're stuck, start by thinking about how the writer is directing your attention.

Sentence Forms

Writing about the effects of different sentence forms will earn you marks in questions about both structure and language, so it's well worth reading up on the next two pages. You'll be a sentence pro by the time you're done.

Sentences are made up of clauses

1) A <u>clause</u> is a part of a sentence that has a <u>subject</u> and a <u>verb</u>. A clause will usually <u>make sense</u> on its own.

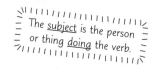
The <u>subject</u> is the person or thing <u>doing</u> the verb.

2) A <u>single clause</u> on its own is called a <u>simple sentence</u>.

The sky was grey and sombre.	This is a single clause that is also a simple sentence. It has a <u>subject</u> ('The sky') and a <u>verb</u> ('was').

3) Simple sentences can be used to <u>explain</u> something <u>clearly</u> and <u>simply</u>. They are also often used to create a <u>sharp</u> or <u>abrupt</u> tone that keeps the reader <u>engaged</u> or creates <u>tension</u>.

4) A <u>compound sentence</u> has <u>two</u> main clauses, linked by a <u>conjunction</u> like 'or', 'but' or 'and'. <u>Both</u> clauses have to be able to make sense on their own. For example:

The sky was grey and sombre, and the rain lashed at our faces.	Writers can use compound sentences to do things like <u>expand</u> on their initial statement, creating more <u>detailed</u> and <u>interesting</u> descriptions.

5) <u>Complex sentences</u> have <u>two</u> or more clauses, but only <u>one</u> of them needs to make sense on its own.

Above the sleepy town, the sky was grey and sombre.	This is a complex sentence — 'Above the sleepy town' wouldn't work as a sentence on its <u>own</u>. This clause could go either <u>before</u> or <u>after</u> the main clause. Writers often <u>create interest</u> by using complex sentences to break up the <u>rhythm</u> of a text.

6) Writers use a variety of <u>sentence forms</u> to achieve different <u>effects</u> and keep the reader <u>interested</u>.

There are four main types of sentence

1) Different <u>types</u> of sentences have different <u>purposes</u>:

- <u>Statements</u> deliver <u>information</u>, e.g. 'The referee made the decision.' They can be found in all texts, but they are particularly common in <u>informative</u> texts like newspaper articles, reports and reviews.

- <u>Questions</u> ask the reader something, e.g. 'What would you do in my situation?' They don't always require an <u>answer</u> — sometimes they are just there to <u>encourage</u> us to <u>think</u> about something.

- <u>Orders</u>, or <u>commands</u>, tell us to <u>do</u> something, e.g. 'Consider the effects of this in the long term.' They often use <u>imperative</u> verbs (verbs that give an instruction, like 'remember', 'think about' or 'go').

- <u>Exclamations</u> convey <u>strong emotions</u>, e.g. 'This is outrageous!' or 'This cannot be allowed to continue!' They usually end with an <u>exclamation mark</u>, and they're common in <u>persuasive</u> texts.

2) For the <u>reading questions</u>, it's a good idea to think about <u>how</u> and <u>why</u> writers have used particular <u>types</u> of sentence — bear in mind that different sentence types are suited to different <u>purposes</u>.

Sentence Forms

Writers use different sentence forms to interest the reader

1) Varying the <u>length</u> of sentences can create different <u>effects</u>. Here are a couple of <u>examples</u>:

> These are just examples — the effects of different sentence lengths will vary from text to text.

> *The sky was growing darker. I couldn't see where I was going. I stumbled.*
>
> → Short simple sentences can be used to <u>build tension</u> or to create a <u>worried</u> and <u>confused</u> tone.

> *I waited excitedly at the foot of the stairs, listening to the footsteps above, thinking about the afternoon ahead, pacing the hall and counting down the minutes until we could set off.*
>
> → A longer, complex sentence could be used to give the impression of <u>time dragging</u>.

2) The <u>order</u> of words within sentences can also be chosen to create an <u>effect</u>. For example:

> *I had <u>never</u> seen such chaos <u>before</u>.*
>
> *<u>Never before</u> had I seen such chaos.*
>
> → Writers sometimes use <u>inversion</u> (<u>altering</u> the normal <u>word order</u>) to change the <u>emphasis</u> in a text. Here, inversion helps to emphasise the phrase '<u>Never before</u>'.

3) If you notice something about the way a writer has used sentences, don't just identify it — you need to <u>analyse</u> the <u>effects</u> to show how they <u>influence</u> the reader.

Comment on the effects of different sentence forms

PAPER 1

A3. What impression do you get of the narrator's feelings from these lines?

This is a long sentence that leaves the reader breathless by the end. It emphasises the feeling of weariness that the narrator is describing.

The repetition in the sentence beginnings 'My heart began', 'My hands began' and 'My mind began' gives emphasis to the physical effects of the narrator's fear.

Short, simple sentences are used to reinforce the narrator's feelings of dread.

The use of a colon shows that there is going to be some form of explanation. This highlights the move away from unexplained short simple sentences.

This longer sentence marks a change in tone from fear to anger.

This inversion disrupts the usual word order and focuses the reader's attention on the narrator's anger.

> It was late evening by the time I returned home from the shops, tired and weary from barging my way past all the desperate Christmas Eve shoppers. It had been a long day, and I was ready for a relaxing bath and a long sleep. It wasn't until I was halfway up the path that I noticed the front door was ajar. My heart began beating wildly inside my chest as I hesitantly advanced towards the door. My hands began to shake. My mind began conjuring apparitions of the unspeakable horrors that could be lurking inside. On reaching the door, I took a deep breath, collected my senses and stepped across the threshold. Everything was quiet and still. I crossed the hall and put down my shopping. Everything looked normal. Nothing was out of place. Suddenly I heard a noise above me. Someone was upstairs. I gasped. But then a change came over me: my fear had turned to resolute anger. Seldom had I experienced such intense fury in all my life. There was an intruder in my house, and they had no right to be there. I made for the stairs.

Phew, there's a lot to get your clause into on these pages...

This stuff's pretty complex (see what I did there...), but it's worth spending some time on it — it'll really help you in the language and structure questions if you can talk about the effects of different sentence forms.

Presentation

The exams are mostly focused on the effects of language and structure, but some texts may also have presentational features that you could comment on. Here's a bit of information to help you with that...

Think about the effect of pictures

Captions are sometimes used to add humour to pictures, although this one is doing a pretty poor job.

1) Texts often use <u>pictures</u> to <u>illustrate</u> what they're about.

2) Sometimes pictures are used to emphasise a <u>feeling</u>. For example, photos of the effects of war make us see how <u>horrible</u> it must be.

3) Pictures can be specially <u>selected</u> to emphasise <u>one particular feeling</u> instead of others. E.g. a writer could make sure there are no <u>hopeful</u> photos of people being rescued in a war — that way we're <u>only shown</u> how horrible it is.

4) Pictures often have <u>captions</u> with them — a short bit of text that helps the reader to <u>understand</u> what the picture shows.

Headlines and subheadings help to focus the reader's attention

1) Headlines tell you, very <u>briefly</u>, what a newspaper or magazine article is <u>about</u>.

2) They try to capture the reader's <u>interest</u>, so that the reader <u>wants</u> to continue reading the text. To do this, they might use <u>humour</u> or language techniques such as <u>onomatopoeia</u> or <u>hyperbole</u>:

MEMBERS MOURN AS CRICKET CLUB CREMATED *Residents of Halsington are said to be "in shock" after a major fire swept through the cricket club.*	⟹ This headline uses <u>alliteration</u> and the <u>semantic field</u> of <u>funerals</u> (see p.28) to grab the reader's <u>attention</u> and make the article seem <u>interesting</u>.

3) <u>Subheadings</u> can be used to <u>split</u> a text up, so that the material is presented in <u>smaller</u> sections that are easier for the reader to <u>take in</u>.

Have a look at the next page for some examples of subheadings.

4) Subheadings aim to <u>summarise</u> a part of the text, so they're usually quite <u>concise</u>, but they can also be <u>interesting</u> or <u>funny</u>, which encourages the reader to continue reading.

Bullet points and numbered lists break information up

1) <u>Bullet points</u> and <u>numbered lists</u> are often used when writers want to give you <u>lots of information</u>, e.g. when writing to <u>advise</u> or <u>inform</u>.

2) They separate complex information into <u>concise</u> points to make it easier to <u>understand</u> and <u>remember</u>.

3) Numbered lists are most commonly used when information needs to be read in a <u>specific order</u>:

1. Preheat the oven to 200°C. *2. Mix the butter, eggs, sugar and flour in a large bowl.* *3. Pour the mixture into a cake tin and bake until golden brown.*	⟹ This uses <u>numbered points</u> to give step-by-step instructions that are <u>easy</u> for the reader to <u>follow</u>.

4) Bullet points are often used when the order of the points <u>isn't as important</u>.

To stay healthy, you need to: • *Drink plenty of water.* • *Eat lots of fruit and vegetables.*	⟹ It doesn't <u>matter</u> what <u>order</u> these points are in, but the <u>bullet points</u> break the information up <u>clearly</u> so it stands out to the reader.

Presentation

Write about how presentation affects the reader

PAPER 2

A2. The author of this magazine article is trying to persuade the reader to exercise more. How does she try to do this?

This uses a title to immediately suggest to the reader that keeping fit is 'easy'.

Interesting subheadings are used to organise the text and hold the reader's interest.

KEEPING FIT — THE EASY WAY

Exercise is important for your health, but nowadays our time and budget are often limited. Fortunately, there are many cheap, simple and fun ways to keep fit.

WALK THE WALK

Walking costs you nothing, and it doesn't require too much spare time. You could try:

- Walking to a friend's house instead of asking for a lift.
- Planning a longer route to a destination you already walk to.
- Getting off the bus or train a few stops early and walking the rest of the way.

PEDAL POWER

If you own a bike, cycling is an excellent way to keep fit. Look at your council's website to see if there are cycle routes nearby, or plan a safe route on your local roads.

DANCE THE NIGHT AWAY

Dancing can help to maintain your fitness and improve your coordination, regardless of your skill level. Try looking for tutorial videos on the Internet or local classes to help you learn something new.

YOUR TURN...

These are just a few ideas; there are many more options available. Whether it's skipping, skating or salsa, there will certainly be something for you.

Bullet points are used to break the information up for the reader, making it more accessible.

This includes a picture, which adds interest for the reader and illustrates a point being made in the text.

This explains why the text's presentation is significant.

The writer uses a short headline to introduce the article and draw attention to the idea that keeping fit can be "easy". The title is also set in capital letters and bold type, so that the idea really stands out. This might persuade the reader to exercise more by immediately and clearly suggesting that it isn't too difficult to do.

The article also includes an appealing image of a cyclist at sunset, which helps to persuade the reader by suggesting that cycling is a pleasant activity that they would enjoy doing. The image also breaks up the text, which makes the article look more interesting and less intimidating. This might encourage the reader to continue reading the article and therefore make them more likely to be persuaded to exercise more.

Remember to link your points back to the question.

You don't need to give a detailed description of a picture — just make it clear how it affects the reader.

A picture isn't always worth a thousand words...

Be careful when writing about presentational devices. It's good to discuss them in your answer — just don't get carried away describing the details of a picture when you could be analysing the effect it has.

Section Three — Reading: Language and Structure

Writing with Purpose

All writing has a purpose — even this introduction, which is here to explain that this page is about purpose.

Structure your writing to suit your purpose

See pages 15-19 for more about writer's purpose.

1) The purpose of your writing might be to <u>inform</u>, <u>advise</u>, <u>argue</u> or <u>persuade</u>, or <u>entertain</u>. It could even be <u>more than one</u> of these.

2) For paper 1, you'll be asked to write <u>creatively</u>, so your purpose should be to <u>entertain</u>.

3) For paper 2, the purpose might be <u>obvious</u>, e.g. you could be asked to write a letter to <u>advise</u> the reader. It can be <u>less obvious</u> though, e.g. you might be asked to "share your views" on a topic, which you could do by writing to <u>argue</u> or <u>persuade</u>.

4) Different purposes will need different <u>structures</u>, so you'll need to think about a <u>structure</u> that will help you achieve your purpose most effectively.

5) You can lay out your structure by writing a <u>plan</u>, so that it stays <u>consistent</u> throughout your answer:

In this case, your purpose is to argue, so you'll need a structure that sets out your argument effectively.

B2. Write an article for your school newspaper arguing in favour or against the way teenagers are portrayed in the media.

PLAN

Stating your point of view clearly at the start of your answer helps to give your article a clear direction.

1) *State the problem — negative image of teens in media, changes way teens are perceived, breaks down links between generations.*

You could present an opposing argument and explain why it's wrong...

2) *Give an example of an unfair news report, explain why it's not fair — not representative of all teens, exaggerates the truth.*

... then use a contrasting argument to explain your own viewpoint.

3) *Give some positive examples of teenagers to contrast negative examples, explain that they're more accurate / representative.*

Choose your tone, style and register to match your purpose

See p.25-26 for more on tone, style and register.

1) In order to get good marks, you also need to show that you can <u>adjust</u> your <u>tone</u>, <u>style</u> and <u>register</u> to suit your purpose.

2) For example, an <u>informative</u> text might have a <u>serious</u>, <u>reserved</u> style, with a <u>formal</u> register:

The UK's younger generation show signs of frustration at the way they are perceived. Studies show that up to 95% of 18-24 year-olds feel that their stance on environmentalism is being ignored. → This text uses <u>technical terms</u> and <u>statistics</u> to help clearly inform the reader.

3) A <u>persuasive</u> text needs to be more <u>subjective</u> (based on personal feelings). It might use rhetorical techniques (see p.35) to create a <u>personal</u> tone that involves the reader in a text:

Like me, you must be weary of the incessant criticism. We're intelligent young citizens who understand the issues threatening our planet. Why are we being ignored? → This text uses a <u>rhetorical question</u> and the pronouns 'you' and 'we' to <u>involve</u> and <u>persuade</u> its audience.

4) When you adjust your <u>writing</u> to suit your purpose, make sure you're still showing off your ability to use <u>sophisticated vocabulary</u>.

Writing with Purpose

Fiction texts are often written to entertain

PAPER 1

*In this section you will be assessed for the quality of your **creative prose writing** skills.*

Choose **one** of the following titles for your writing:

Either, (a) Finding Inspiration.
Or, (b) Old Friends.
Or, (c) Write about a time when you felt frightened.
Or, (d) Write a story which begins:
    I'd never been so far away from home before...

> You're writing a piece of fiction, so you need to entertain the reader.

FINDING INSPIRATION

I'd never in my life needed a break so badly. My airless writing room had begun to feel suffocating; so had the frustration of my unending writer's block. I gave up, threw down my pen, and went out for a walk.

My irritation evaporated almost immediately into the crisp autumn air. Buoyed by the hope of finding inspiration amongst the fiery leaves that surrounded me, I ambled contentedly through the silence of the golden wood.

> This story starts in the middle of the action to grab the reader's interest.

> Unusual vocabulary makes your writing more interesting and enjoyable to read.

> This uses complex sentences to keep the writing style varied.

> Figurative language helps the reader to imagine the writer's feelings.

Non-fiction texts can have a variety of purposes

PAPER 2

B2. You have read a magazine article which claims that cosmetic surgery is needless and should be banned.

You have decided to write an article for your local newspaper to share your views on this idea. You could write in favour or against this idea.

Write a lively article for the newspaper giving your views.

> In this task, your purpose is to explain your point of view — you could do this by writing to argue.

Public consensus has long seen cosmetic surgery as a mere vanity project, a procedure dreamed up by the wealthy to aid their endless pursuit of perfection. This seems somewhat unfair on the medical establishment.

In truth, cosmetic surgery sits at the height of medical achievement. Far from being a symptom of a shallow society, cosmetic procedures are a solution: they offer the chance of a new life. Plastic surgery has the power to improve lives, something that has always been an important medical objective.

It is time for a sea-change in attitudes to plastic surgery — it is no longer acceptable for the world to view with scorn those who have chosen to specialise in the improvement of the human form.

> If you're writing to argue, you could structure your answer by stating an opposing opinion and then counteracting it.

> Emotive phrases like this can help to make the audience agree with your viewpoint.

> You need to use a confident, assured tone to make your argument convincing.

This revision guide's purpose is to get you through your exams...

Don't forget that writing can often have more than one purpose — make sure you think about all the reasons that you're writing, so that you can adapt your style and produce a top-quality piece of writing. Easy peasy.

Writing for an Audience

For each writing task, you'll need to bear in mind your audience. Your audience is just anyone who's going to hear or read your writing — it doesn't mean you'll have to perform your work to a room full of strangers...

Work out who the audience is for your writing

1) For the writing questions on both papers, you'll need to write in a way that suits your audience.

2) In paper 1, your creative writing will need to appeal to a general, adult audience.

3) In paper 2, a question might specify a particular audience:

> **B1.** Your local council wants to improve how eco-friendly they are.
>
> **Write a report for the members of your local council suggesting ways this might be done.**

Here's the audience — 'the members of your local council'.

4) However, you might need to work out who your audience is, using clues from the question. The form might give you some ideas:

You're writing a broadsheet newspaper article, so your audience will mostly be well-educated adults.

> **B2.** You have read a report which claims that students should attend school virtually instead of in person.
>
> **Write an article to be published in a broadsheet newspaper giving your views on this idea.**

Choose your tone, style and register to match your audience

1) Once you know who your audience is, you'll need to adapt your tone, style and register so that they're appropriate to the people who will be reading your writing.

See p.25-26 for more on tone, style and register.

2) For example, you might want to consider the age and level of expertise of your audience, as well as your relationship with them.

Age

- If you're addressing a younger audience, you might use a more light-hearted tone and an informal register, with a colloquial or chatty style.

- A formal, serious register that doesn't use any slang might work better for older audiences. You might also use a more complex style than you would for a younger audience.

Expertise

- Different audiences will have different levels of expertise in the subject you're writing about.

- For example, if you're writing a report for a panel of experts, your register should be more formal, with a style that uses more specialised language than if you were writing for a general audience.

Relationship with reader

- If you're writing to a familiar audience, like a friend, you might use an informal register, and a friendly tone.

- If you're writing to an unknown audience, it would be better to use an impersonal tone and a formal register.

3) You should always aim to show your writing skills to the examiner — even if you're writing informally or for a young audience, you still need to make sure you include a range of vocabulary and sentence types.

Writing for an Audience

Fiction texts need to engage their audience

*In this section you will be assessed for the quality of your **creative prose writing** skills.*

Choose **one** of the following titles for your writing:

PAPER 1

The writing question in paper 1 won't give a specific audience, so you need to make sure that your writing appeals to a general, adult audience.

Either, *(a)* The New Shoes.
Or, *(b)* Write about a birthday party.

You'll be given four options in the real exam.

Try surprising your audience with something unexpected, e.g. addressing the reader directly.

Amelia's eighteenth birthday had truly been a day like no other. It was the day she first met Jack: a tall, handsome stranger dressed in a naval uniform.

Don't be fooled by the intrusion of a charming stranger into this narrative. This is not a romance novel, and Amelia was not Cinderella. Jack was her brother — her long-lost brother, who had left to join the Navy before she had been born, and who returned now with the despondence of a disgraced man.

Amelia could never forget her mother's face as she had opened the door to greet another well-wishing neighbour, only to find her lost son hunched on the doorstep. Her features appeared to melt, losing all definition as they formed themselves into a canvas over which several emotions flashed. At first there was shock, which quickly became anger, then relief, and finally, remorse.

An unusual image like this makes the text interesting for the audience.

Non-fiction texts can use a personal tone

PAPER 2

B1. Your school is worried about the dangers of online bullying.

Write a speech to be given at your school advising teenagers on how to cope with online bullying.

In this task, you're writing for a teenage audience, so you'll need to adjust your tone, style and register accordingly.

You're writing to advise teenagers. Use words like "we" and "us" to establish a connection and give your advice calmly, without being patronising.

Your tone should be helpful and friendly, but in this case your register should still be quite formal. Don't use any slang or text speak.

Every day, most of us use some form of social media to broadcast our identities. We're telling the world, "This is who I am." That's why cyber-bullying, whether it's a public post on social media or a private email from an anonymous source, can be so upsetting — it can feel like your whole identity is being attacked.

There are many different ways to deal with online bullying. The first thing you need to do is report it. You can usually do this on the website itself, but if you don't feel comfortable doing this, you should talk to someone in person.

If you find you are the victim of persistent bullying, take steps to block the person who is bullying you from contacting you. It's also a good idea to record the bullying in some way — you could take a screenshot, or even just save the messages somewhere. This will make things much easier to report later.

I don't believe it, she's written an essay! And the crowd goes wild!

You'll be pleased to hear that your audience won't actually be there in the exam room — although I suppose it might be nice to have a group of people to applaud you whenever you craft a particularly good sentence...

Creative Writing

You need to do some creative writing for paper 1, which might sound a bit scary. Never fear — whack in some descriptive language, a thrilling narrative plot and an interesting character or two, and you won't go far wrong.

Grab your reader's attention from the start

1) It's always a good idea to <u>start</u> your writing with an <u>opening sentence</u> that'll make your <u>reader</u> want to <u>carry on</u> reading. For example:

You could start with a <u>direct address</u> to the reader:

> *Everybody has a bad day now and again, don't they? Well, I'm going to tell you about a day that was much, much worse than your worst day ever.*

Grabbing attention had never been a problem for Marvin.

Or you could try a description of a particularly <u>unusual character</u>:

> *Humphrey Ward was, without a shadow of a doubt, the most brilliant (and most cantankerous) banana thief in the country.*

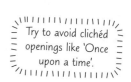

Try to avoid clichéd openings like 'Once upon a time'.

2) If you start your writing in the <u>middle of the action</u>, it'll create a <u>fast-paced</u> atmosphere that makes the reader want to find out <u>what happens next</u>:

> *I couldn't believe it. He was gone. "He must be here," I thought to myself as I went through the shed, desperately throwing aside box after box. It was no use. Peter had run away, and it was all my fault.*

3) This example <u>explains</u> some of what's happening after a few sentences, which keeps up the <u>fast pace</u> of the narrative — so the text stays <u>interesting</u>.

4) You could also try <u>prolonging</u> the mystery to create <u>tension</u> in your narrative. Just make sure you <u>reveal</u> what's going on before it gets <u>confusing</u>.

5) However you start your writing, you need to make sure it's <u>engaging</u> and <u>entertaining</u> for the reader — so use interesting <u>language</u> and don't <u>waffle</u>.

Try to build the tension from the start

PAPER 1

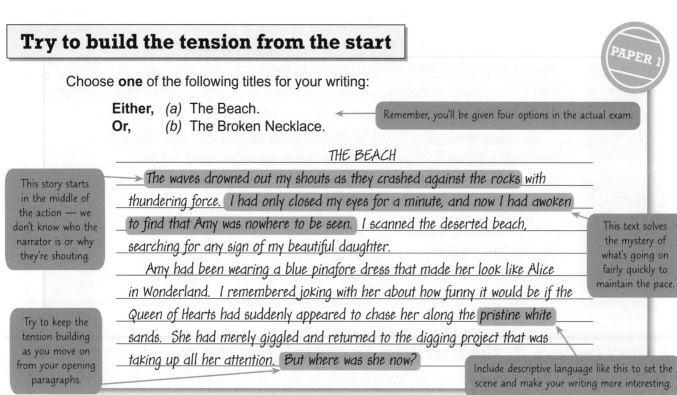

Choose **one** of the following titles for your writing:

Either, *(a)* The Beach.
Or, *(b)* The Broken Necklace.

Remember, you'll be given four options in the actual exam.

THE BEACH

The waves drowned out my shouts as they crashed against the rocks with thundering force. I had only closed my eyes for a minute, and now I had awoken to find that Amy was nowhere to be seen. I scanned the deserted beach, searching for any sign of my beautiful daughter.

Amy had been wearing a blue pinafore dress that made her look like Alice in Wonderland. I remembered joking with her about how funny it would be if the Queen of Hearts had suddenly appeared to chase her along the pristine white sands. She had merely giggled and returned to the digging project that was taking up all her attention. But where was she now?

This story starts in the middle of the action — we don't know who the narrator is or why they're shouting.

This text solves the mystery of what's going on fairly quickly to maintain the pace.

Try to keep the tension building as you move on from your opening paragraphs.

Include descriptive language like this to set the scene and make your writing more interesting.

Creative Writing

Make your language and narrative viewpoint fit the task

1) Different <u>word choices</u> will have different <u>effects</u>, so you'll need to pick vocabulary that creates the right <u>tone</u> for your story. For example:

> *The door screeched open and I carefully entered the dingy cellar. Shadows cast by my torch leapt up at me through the gloom.*

Words like '<u>screeched</u>', '<u>dingy</u>' and '<u>gloom</u>' make this writing sound <u>spooky</u>.

> *I burst noisily through the thicket of trees and sprinted towards the shore. The men were still chasing me, bellowing threats.*

Words like '<u>burst</u>', '<u>sprinted</u>' and '<u>chasing</u>' make this writing sound <u>exciting</u> and <u>dramatic</u>.

2) You also need to think about what <u>narrative viewpoint</u> you're going to use (see p.38).

3) A <u>first-person narrator</u> uses the pronouns 'I' and 'we', as they're usually one of the <u>characters</u> in the story.

> *I quickly scanned the book for anything that might help. My heart was racing; I knew I needed to work fast.*

The first-person narrative makes things more <u>dramatic</u> by helping the reader to <u>imagine</u> the story is happening to them.

4) A <u>third-person narrator</u> uses words like 'he' and 'she' to talk <u>about</u> the characters from a <u>separate</u> viewpoint.

> *Shamil lit the bonfire carefully, then retreated back a few metres as the feeble fire began to crackle and spit.*

The narrator isn't part of the story. This creates <u>distance</u>, as the narrative voice and the characters are <u>separate</u> from each other.

Use descriptive techniques to make your text engaging

Choose **one** of the following titles for your writing:

Either, *(a)* Write about a time when you visited a friend.
Or, *(b)* The Camp.

It's important to show off your descriptive skills to the examiner — interesting vocabulary and imagery can help you achieve this.

THE CAMP

The sun dipped low beneath the looming, dusky sky. Its daytime glory was reduced to the fading flicker of a tiny ember that only just protruded above the dark horizon. Down in the valley, the camp hummed with activity: people milled about like ants, erecting tents, cooking meals and tending the fire, the smoke from which crept stealthily up the side of the mound, eventually reaching the rider's nostrils and filling him with the warming aromas of home.

A glance beyond the confines of the camp revealed the open plains beyond, as they bathed in the warmth of the dying light. Come nightfall, these plains would transform from places of refuge into discordant wastelands, answerable only to the laws of nature.

Using figurative language, like similes and personification, will help to make your text more engaging.

This text uses a third-person narrator, so the narrative isn't limited to the rider's perspective.

Combine visual imagery with other senses to help the reader imagine they are there with the narrator.

Creative Writing

It's important to write a good ending

1) It's important that you <u>finish</u> your writing well — you want to leave the examiner with a <u>great impression</u> of your writing abilities.

2) Here are some <u>examples</u> of different ways that you could <u>end</u> your writing:

> - You could finish with an unexpected <u>plot twist</u> that will <u>shock</u> the reader.
> - You could show the <u>main character</u> coming to some kind of <u>realisation</u>.
> - You could create a <u>cliffhanger</u> ending by finishing with a <u>question</u>. This will leave the reader thinking about what will happen <u>next</u>.
> - You could have a <u>neat</u>, <u>happy ending</u> that will <u>satisfy</u> the reader.

Buster had come to the realisation that he was going to need a haircut.

3) If you find you're running out of time, think up a <u>quick ending</u> — make sure you show how the story ends, and finish with a short, <u>punchy</u> line.

Under absolutely no circumstances use the ending, "And it was all a dream."

Try to make your ending as powerful as possible

PAPER 1

Choose **one** of the following titles for your writing:

Either, *(a)* The Decision.
Or, *(b)* The House on the Hill.

THE DECISION

... I knew I should never have stolen the vase. It had been a moment of madness. I had just seen it sitting there, and it looked so beautiful and elegant. All of my problems stemmed from that decision, that single flash of foolishness. I spent a long time wondering what to do with the vase. I studied it intently. It was too beautiful to discard, too dazzling to keep concealed any longer. Eventually, I made a decision. I took it to the cliff and threw it over, watching it smash on the rocks below. It was an awful sight, but at least my guilty secret was gone forever.

Late that night, the wind was howling around my tent, and the rain was pelting down on the canvas. Suddenly, there was a huge crash of thunder and a blinding flash of lightning. Terrified, I ran out of the tent, only to be greeted by a strange apparition: there, sitting on top of a tree stump, was the missing vase. It was completely whole. Not a single crack was visible on its smooth, shiny exterior. I whirled around and scoured the field for any sign of an intruder. That was when I saw the old, hunched man walking slowly away.

This is just the ending of a story — your answer in the exam would have several paragraphs building up to this point.

You should build the tension towards a climax that will resolve the action.

After you've given a satisfying ending, you could go on to add an unexpected twist that leaves the reader with doubt in their mind.

However you end your text, make sure it's exciting and powerful.

"It was all a dream" — the examiner's nightmare...

Seriously — steer as far away as you can from clichéd endings. All they do is prove to the examiner that you haven't thought very hard about your answer, as well as being less interesting than queuing for the toilet.

Section Four — Writing: Creative and Non-Fiction

Writing Articles

Articles are non-fiction texts found in newspapers, magazines or on the Internet that are used to convey information, ideas or opinions to the reader. Have a look at the next three pages to find out more...

Articles report events and offer opinions

1) The main purpose of most articles is to <u>inform</u> people about <u>current affairs</u> or <u>other topics</u> of interest.

2) They do this in <u>two main ways</u>:

By directly reporting information

- Some articles are written to convey <u>facts</u> about a <u>story</u> or <u>theme</u>.

- They may report the viewpoints of <u>other people</u>, but the writer will not directly express their <u>own viewpoint</u> on the subject.

- The writer's <u>own viewpoint</u> might come across through the viewpoints of the people they <u>choose to quote</u>.

By writing commentaries

- Commentaries (also called <u>columns</u>, <u>editorials</u> or <u>opinion pieces</u>) offer the <u>viewpoint</u> of the <u>writer</u> on a news story or an important theme.

- Commentaries <u>entertain</u> their audience, as readers engage with the <u>personality</u> of the writer by <u>agreeing</u> or <u>disagreeing</u> with their opinions and insights.

Articles need to engage their audience

1) If an article is <u>only</u> trying to convey facts, the writer will usually use an <u>unemotional tone</u>.

2) The register may be <u>technical</u> and the style quite <u>sophisticated</u>, in order to make the information seem <u>accurate</u> and <u>reliable</u>.

> *The author of the controversial report, Professor Hyde, has stated that, "agricultural reform is necessary to build a sustainable future". The report has, however, attracted widespread criticism from members of the agricultural community.*

This conveys information in a <u>direct</u> way, using an <u>impersonal</u> tone, and with sophisticated, precise vocabulary. Viewpoints are conveyed by <u>quoting</u> and <u>paraphrasing</u>.

3) A commentary might use a <u>personal</u> tone and a <u>conversational</u> style to help convey the writer's <u>opinions</u> and <u>personality</u>.

> *It seems to me that this lot all need to take a deep breath and stop whinging. Nobody's going to bulldoze our green spaces any time soon — they'll have to spend 25 years making a planning application first.*

This uses <u>colloquial</u> words to create a conversational style and <u>sarcasm</u> to convey the viewpoint of the writer.

4) <u>Rhetorical techniques</u> (see p.35) are commonly used in commentaries to help get the writer's opinions across forcefully and to encourage readers to <u>agree</u> with the writer.

> *What happened to the good old days, when the presence of a heap of spuds on the table at dinnertime brought delight all round? Has all this 'health food' nonsense made us forget our faithful starchy friend?*

This uses <u>rhetorical questions</u> to engage and persuade the reader.

Writing Articles

The layout of an article is important

Articles often use <u>layout features</u> to engage the reader's <u>attention</u> and convey information <u>clearly</u>.

Headlines tell you, very briefly, what an article is about. Headlines need to capture the audience's interest so that they carry on reading the article. They might use techniques like alliteration or humour to achieve this.

Subheadings are used to split an article up. Each subheading briefly tells you what the next section of text is about, often in an interesting or humorous way.

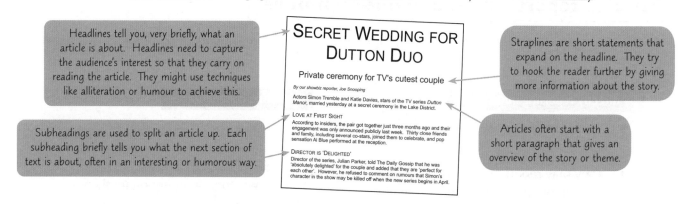

SECRET WEDDING FOR DUTTON DUO

Private ceremony for TV's cutest couple

By our showbiz reporter, Joe Snooping

Actors Simon Tremble and Katie Davies, stars of the TV series *Dutton Manor*, married yesterday at a secret ceremony in the Lake District.

LOVE AT FIRST SIGHT
According to insiders, the pair got together just three months ago and their engagement was only announced publicly last week. Thirty close friends and family, including several co-stars, joined them to celebrate, and pop sensation Al Blue performed at the reception.

DIRECTOR IS 'DELIGHTED'
Director of the series, Julian Parker, told The Daily Gossip that he was 'absolutely delighted' for the couple and added that they are 'perfect for each other'. However, he refused to comment on rumours that Simon's character in the show may be killed off when the new series begins in April.

Straplines are short statements that expand on the headline. They try to hook the reader further by giving more information about the story.

Articles often start with a short paragraph that gives an overview of the story or theme.

Newspapers are aimed at a general audience

1) A newspaper's main purpose is to <u>inform</u> people about <u>current affairs</u> and <u>other topics</u> that people are interested in.

2) Newspapers are mostly made up of informative <u>news reports</u>, although they also have <u>commentaries</u> that give the writer's <u>viewpoint</u> on a particular news story.

3) Most newspapers are aimed at a <u>wide</u>, <u>adult</u> audience, although they might <u>target</u> their articles towards a particular <u>political viewpoint</u> or <u>social class</u>.

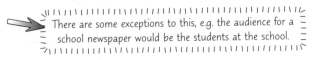

There are some exceptions to this, e.g. the audience for a school newspaper would be the students at the school.

4) Newspapers are broadly split into two types — <u>tabloids</u> and <u>broadsheets</u>.

- <u>Tabloids</u> (such as *The Sun* and *The Mirror*) tend to focus on more <u>sensational</u> topics and people, making their news stories accessible and with a wide appeal.

- <u>Broadsheets</u> (such as *The Telegraph* and *The Guardian*) are thought of as more <u>formal</u>, 'high-brow' journalism — focusing on what are thought to be more sophisticated topics.

Magazines are often about a special interest

1) <u>Magazines</u> usually focus on a particular <u>activity or interest</u>, such as fishing or art.

2) This means they need to appeal to their <u>particular audience</u>. This can be a <u>wide</u> audience, e.g. a magazine aimed at all women, or a more <u>specific</u> audience, e.g. a community magazine aimed at residents of a particular area.

I'd recommend some hardy perennials, such as peonies, which can provide a flash of much-needed colour during late spring and early summer.

This text has a <u>specific</u> audience — it's aimed at people who are interested in <u>gardening</u>. It uses <u>specialist</u> language to convey the <u>writer's viewpoint</u> in an authoritative way.

3) Magazines tend to focus on <u>entertaining</u> the reader, so they will contain mostly <u>commentaries</u> — although some articles will be written purely to <u>inform</u> the reader.

Section Four — Writing: Creative and Non-Fiction

Writing Articles

Internet articles can be aimed at any audience

1) You might also be asked to write an article to be published <u>online</u>. This could be <u>either</u> a commentary <u>or</u> a news report.

2) Internet articles can have <u>any</u> purpose. This often depends on exactly <u>where</u> they're published — an article published on the website for a <u>broadsheet newspaper</u> could be purely <u>informative</u>, but an entry for a <u>blog</u> is likely to be written in a more <u>argumentative</u> way.

3) The audience for an online article might be <u>different</u> to that of traditional media, e.g. <u>younger</u> or with a different level of <u>understanding</u> about a subject.

4) Even though you're writing for an <u>online</u> audience, you should always use <u>Standard English</u> and avoid <u>abbreviations</u> or <u>smiley faces</u>.

Edith took the "no smiley faces" rule very seriously.

Think about the tone of your article

PAPER 2

B2. You have a friend who claims that guided tours don't allow tourists to see the true heart of a country.

You have decided to write an article for a travel magazine to share your views on this idea. You could agree or disagree with their opinion.

This question is asking you to give your opinion on a topic.

Write a lively article for the magazine giving your views.

Your headline needs to be short and punchy to engage the reader.

FORGET THE ROAD LESS TRAVELLED

Guided tours are the best way to experience somewhere new.

Use a strapline to summarise the article in an interesting way.

You're giving an opinion, so your tone should be quite personal.

At some point or other, we've all encountered a travel snob: that particular breed of traveller who knows all about where to go, what to see and, most importantly, how to see it. The travel snob thinks that guided tours are for uncultured bores. The travel snob believes in travel without a destination. And yet, the travel snob will always find time to tell you about a 'hidden gem' that only they can take you to.

Use rhetorical devices like repetition to make your writing entertaining.

You can use a sarcastic tone to give your writing a sense of personality.

You would think someone so worldly-wise would see the irony — travel snobs are themselves tour guides. Their cherished 'off the beaten track' spots are transported, by their recommendation, right onto 'the beaten track' — they're the ones beating it, leading tourists away from well-known honeypot sites and into 'the heart of things'.

Make sure you link your answer to the prompt you're given in the question.

Opinion articles often combine a relatively informal style with complex sentences and vocabulary.

In the meantime, guided tours are often run by local people, who will frequently have a real treasure trove of local knowledge. How can a throwaway recommendation from an outsider possibly surpass that? Anybody who wants to see the true heart of a country must be guided by the people who live in it.

"Why do you prefer broad sheets?" "I've got a really wide bed..."

It's worth having a look at some real articles from different sources as part of your revision. You'll soon start to spot patterns in the vocabulary and structure that they use, which will help you to write a top-notch answer.

Writing Leaflets

Leaflets need to give the reader lots of information in a clear, organised way.

Leaflets can have varied audiences and purposes

1) Leaflets can have <u>any</u> purpose, but they're often used to <u>advise</u> (e.g. a leaflet advising the reader to open a savings account) or <u>persuade</u> an audience (e.g. to vote for a particular political party).

2) They can have a <u>general audience</u> (e.g. a leaflet about the importance of healthy eating) or a more <u>specific audience</u> (e.g. a leaflet advertising a particular museum or exhibition).

3) Leaflets need a <u>clear structure</u> to <u>break up</u> information. This could include:

> • a clear title   • subheadings   • bullet points

4) Leaflets also need to <u>grab the reader's attention</u>, so that they <u>remember</u> all the information they're given. You can use <u>language techniques</u>, such as <u>lists of three</u> or <u>direct address</u>, to achieve this.

Organise your leaflet in a clear and interesting way

PAPER 2

B1. Your local pet shelter is struggling with the number of animals they have to look after.

Write the text for a leaflet aimed at people in your local area, in which you persuade them to adopt a pet from the local pet shelter.

You could include:

• examples of the types of pet they can adopt;
• reasons to go to the local pet shelter instead of elsewhere.

This addresses the reader in a direct, flattering way, which creates a personal connection that makes the reader more likely to trust the writer.

Use a title to catch the attention of the target audience (people who might want to adopt a pet).

THINKING OF GETTING A PET?

You'll probably have considered the type of pet you want to get, and how you'll find the time to feed and care for it — but have you considered where you'll adopt your pet from?

SHELTERS — THE SENSIBLE OPTION

Use subheadings to organise your answer and summarise your main points clearly.

Most people go straight to a local pet shop without thinking, but it's definitely worth checking pet shelters first. Lots of the animals there have been left homeless through no fault of their own, and they're often friendly and affectionate — and house-trained!

YOUR LOCAL SHELTER NEEDS YOU

Short paragraphs can help to break up the information in a text.

Tinsby Pet Shelter is a small, charity-funded organisation that cares for abandoned and homeless pets in Tinsby and the surrounding area. We currently look after:

Bullet points are used to show that there are lots of different animals available for adoption.

• Dogs   • Rabbits   • Guinea Pigs   • Reptiles
• Cats   • Hamsters   • Birds   • ... and even a frog or two!

Unfortunately, many of these adorable animals will never find a new home. And whilst we do our best to keep them happy and healthy, it's no substitute for a loving full-time owner. So don't wait — visit us today. Your new pet can't wait to meet you!

This emotive sentence persuades the reader by appealing to their feelings.

And here I was thinking a leaflet was a baby leaf...

Leaflets can be written for a wide variety of different audiences. Make sure your leaflet is adapted to the audience you're given in the question by choosing a suitable writing style that uses appropriate language.

Travel Writing

Travel writing needs to really convey your feelings about the place you're writing about.

Travel writing is personal and informal

1) Travel writing is an <u>account</u> of a writer's travels to a specific <u>place</u>.

2) If you're asked to produce some travel writing, you'll need to convey your <u>thoughts</u> and <u>opinions</u> about the place you're writing about, as well as give some <u>information</u> about it.

3) A piece of travel writing can <u>entertain</u> the reader (e.g. if it's in a book or magazine), <u>inform</u> them (e.g. if it's in a travel guide), or <u>persuade</u> them to visit a destination.

4) However, it's usually written for a <u>combination</u> of these purposes, e.g. <u>travel guides</u> are often written to both <u>inform</u> and <u>entertain</u> the reader.

5) Travel writing usually has an <u>informal</u> register and a <u>chatty</u> style, and it's almost always written in the <u>first person</u>. Try to write as if you're having a <u>conversation</u> with the audience, but don't forget to use lots of <u>descriptive techniques</u> too.

The travel brochure had failed to specify exactly what they meant by "transport included".

© Miguel Angelo Silva/iStockphoto.com

Use interesting language to convey your opinions

PAPER 2

B2. You have decided to write an article for a national travel magazine to share your views about a destination you have visited.
You could write in favour or against visiting the destination.

Write an entertaining article for the magazine giving your views.

An interesting, punchy title and strapline can help to grab your audience's attention.

> DISMAYED IN MANHATTAN
>
> Lucy Farthing says "no thanks" to New York.
>
> I've travelled to many cities during my career as a travel writer, and it's fair to say that there are a few I'd rather have avoided. None, however, have quite matched up to the discomfort and sheer frustration I experienced in New York. I suspect my high expectations didn't help. Before embarking on my trip, I'd been regaled with stories from friends and family who'd already visited the place. "It's the city of dreams", I was told; "the best city in the world!"
>
> What I realised instead, somewhere between my fifth cup of overpriced coffee and my fourteenth hour-long queue, was that New York is the city of nightmares. Not only did it feel like the world's busiest city, it felt like the noisiest, too; by the end of my week there I found myself longing for the joys of silence and solitude. Maybe for some, New York is a city where dreams come true, but it was certainly far from the inspiring haven I had hoped to find.

This question asks you to write a magazine article. It needs to be entertaining and informative, and could also persuade the reader to agree with your point of view.

Use personal pronouns like 'I' to make the tone of your writing more personal.

Make your opinion on the destination very clear.

Try to use all five senses to create a sense of the atmosphere of the place.

Use interesting language to make your text more entertaining.

Travel left-ing...   ...Travel right-ing

You don't necessarily have to sing the praises of the place you're writing about. It's fine to have a negative opinion, as long as you express it clearly and use the appropriate language, tone and style for your audience.

58

Writing Reports and Essays

Reports and essays use a similar tone and style, but they do have one difference. Read on for the big reveal...

Reports and essays are similar

1) Reports and essays should be <u>impersonal</u> and <u>objective</u> in tone — you'll need to go through the arguments <u>for</u> and <u>against</u> something, then come to a conclusion that demonstrates your <u>own point of view</u>.

2) Reports and essays should follow a <u>logical structure</u>. They need to have:

> • An <u>introduction</u> that sets up the <u>main theme</u>.
>
> • Well-structured <u>paragraphs</u> covering the <u>strengths</u> and <u>weaknesses</u> of the arguments.
>
> • A <u>conclusion</u> that ties things together and offers <u>your own</u> point of view.

3) The purpose of reports and essays is almost always to <u>inform</u>, but they often <u>advise</u> their audience too.

4) You need to make sure you write for the correct <u>audience</u> — <u>essays</u> usually have quite a <u>general</u> audience, but <u>reports</u> are normally written for a <u>particular</u> person or group of people.

Reports should analyse and advise

PAPER 2

B1. Your school has received a grant to fund extra-curricular activities.

Write a report for the board of governors suggesting how they could spend the money.

You could include:
- examples of extra-curricular activities they could spend the money on;
- your ideas about how the money might best be spent.

At the start, show that you are clearly aware of who your audience is.

You don't need to create any suspense — give your opinion in the introduction.

Phrases like 'on the one hand' show that you have thought about both sides of the argument.

Your language should be very formal and impersonal, but you still need to convey a viewpoint.

In the real answer, you would go on to include several more paragraphs and finish with a conclusion that gives advice.

<u>A Report Into The Possible Uses Of The Extra-Curricular Grant</u>

This report has been commissioned by the board of governors to identify the best use of the funds available for extra-curricular activities at St. Swithins Park Secondary School. Two options have been investigated: the rock-climbing club and the film society. After careful consideration of the evidence collected from various interviews and data analysis, the conclusion has been reached that the film club is the most logical recipient of the funds.

On the one hand, the rock-climbing club appears to be the most obvious choice as it is the most costly to run: the club organises frequent expeditions involving expensive equipment and high travel costs. Having said that, the club does charge a members' fee, which helps to alleviate some of this financial burden.

My school reports certainly covered my weaknesses...

Reports and essays are pretty straightforward when it comes down to it — just make sure that you're being as objective, analytical and formal as possible. It may be a bit boring, but it's a perfect recipe for exam success.

Writing Reviews

Writing a review involves clearly giving your opinion about something. The audience are reading because they're genuinely interested in your opinion, so what you say goes. You have all the power. Mwa ha ha...

Reviews should entertain as well as inform

1) A review is a piece of writing that gives an opinion about how good something is
— it might be a book, a piece of music or even an exhibition.

2) Reviews can appear in lots of different publications. If you have to write a review
in the exam, the question will usually tell you where it's going to appear.

3) The publication where your review appears will affect what kind of audience you're writing for and
how you write. For example, a film review for a teen magazine could be funny and informal, but
a review of a Shakespeare play for a broadsheet newspaper should be serious and informative.

4) You should also pay attention to purpose. Your review could have several different purposes:

- Your review needs to entertain the reader.
- You also need to inform the reader about the thing you're reviewing, based on your own opinion.
- You might also need to advise the reader whether or not to see or do the thing you're reviewing.

5) Don't get too hung up on describing everything in detail — it's more important to give your opinion,
and keep your review engaging by focusing on the interesting bits and using sophisticated language.

Your review needs to give an evaluation

PAPER 2

B2. Imagine you have been to a music concert.

You have decided to write a review for a broadsheet newspaper to share your views
about the concert. You could write about it in a positive or negative way.

Write a review for the newspaper giving your views.

'Music through the Millennium': A Feast for the Ears

*From the moment the audience took their seats, the auditorium was buzzing
with excitement, and they were not to be disappointed. This stunning collection of
classical and contemporary pieces took the audience on an unforgettable journey
through a thousand years of music, from the intense gloom and misery of funeral
marches to the pounding excitement of percussion movements, and the intense joy
of some truly superb symphonies. This was a sonic experience not to be missed: a
congregation of musical heavyweights that each packed a punch strong enough to
knock the emotional stuffing out of even the stoniest of hearts. From start to end,
'Music through the Millennium' was a true schooling in the stirring power of music.*

Make your opinion clear from the start of the review.

Make sure your review is informative as well as entertaining.

This review is for a broadsheet newspaper, so make sure you adapt your writing appropriately — use a formal register with fairly complex language.

Use figurative language to make your review interesting.

I read an article about cheese once — it was a brie-view...

*Reviews are quite a nice thing to write — they're all about your opinions, which means you can go to town on
saying what you think. You should try to express your thoughts clearly, and in a way that entertains the reader.*

Writing Speeches

A speech needs to be powerful and moving. Get it right and you might even reduce your audience to tears...

Speeches need to be dramatic and engaging

1) Speeches are often written to argue or persuade, so they need to have a dramatic, emotional impact on their audience.

2) One way to make a speech persuasive is to give it an effective structure — arrange your points so that they build tension throughout your answer, then end with an emotive or exciting climax.

3) You can use lots of language techniques to make your writing engaging and persuasive:

> *These accusations are hateful, hurtful and humiliating.* → Alliteration and the use of a list of three adjectives make this sound strong and angry.

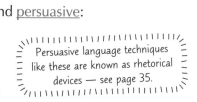
Persuasive language techniques like these are known as rhetorical devices — see page 35.

> *Do we really have no other option? The current situation is a disgrace!* → Rhetorical questions and exclamations engage the reader and make your writing sound more like spoken language.

4) Remember that speeches are spoken, not read. Try to use techniques that are effective when they're spoken out loud.

Your speech should make people think

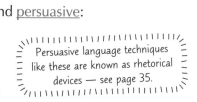
PAPER 2

B2. A proposal has been made to build a new zoo in your local area.

You have decided to make a speech at a local community meeting to share your views on this proposal. You could argue in favour or against this proposal.

Write an engaging speech giving your views.

> Ladies and gentlemen, I am here today to defend the proposal to build a new zoo in Upper Babbleton. I believe that a zoo would be hugely beneficial to our local community.
> Modern British zoos are primarily focused on conservation and education. To my mind, these are important values. We must impress upon the young people of Upper Babbleton the need to protect endangered species and habitats. A zoo can help us to do this. Modern zoos offer extensive opportunities for these kinds of educational experiences: there are interactive exhibitions, talks from conservationists and live question-and-answer forums that will help to educate our young people.
> The new zoo will help us inspire a generation with the importance of conservation. It will help us raise awareness of environmental issues. It will help us by providing a space in which we can work together to build a safer, greener and more ecologically friendly world.

Start off by addressing your listeners directly and announcing the reason for your speech — show that you've understood your purpose and audience.

The word 'must' creates a confident tone.

You could use repetition to increase the dramatic impact of your speech.

Try to use lots of personal pronouns like 'I', 'you' and 'we' to engage your audience.

Vary the lengths of your sentences to show pauses and emphasis.

Use rhetorical devices like lists of three to make your argument sound more forceful.

Ladies, gentlemen, and assorted zoo animals...

There have been loads of famous speeches throughout history — try looking at some of the techniques they use. Luckily for you, your speech doesn't have to impress a huge crowd of people, just a few picky examiners...

Section Four — Writing: Creative and Non-Fiction

Writing Letters

Letters are always addressed to a particular person or group of people. This means that they have very specific audiences, so it's super important that you tailor your letter to suit that audience...

Letters can be formal or informal

1) If you're asked to write a <u>letter</u>, look at the <u>audience</u> to see if you need to use a <u>formal</u> or <u>informal</u> register.

2) If the letter is to someone you <u>don't</u> know well, or to someone in a position of <u>authority</u>, keep it <u>formal</u> with a <u>serious</u> tone. This means you should:

> • Use <u>formal greetings</u> (e.g. 'Dear Sir/Madam') and <u>sign-offs</u> (e.g. 'Yours sincerely' if you've used their name, 'Yours faithfully' if you haven't).
>
> • Use <u>Standard English</u> and <u>formal vocabulary</u>, e.g. you could use phrases like 'In my opinion...' or 'I find this state of affairs...'.

Charlie had forgotten to include a formal sign-off in her letter.

3) If the letter is to a <u>friend</u> or <u>relative</u>, or someone your <u>own</u> age, you should use a more <u>informal</u> register and <u>personal</u> tone. This means you should:

> • Start with your reader's <u>name</u>, e.g. 'Dear Jenny', and <u>sign off</u> with 'best wishes' or 'see you soon'.
>
> • Make sure you still write in <u>Standard English</u> (so no <u>text speak</u> or <u>slang</u>) and show the examiner that you can use interesting <u>vocabulary</u> and <u>sentence structures</u>.

Don't make your letter too chatty

PAPER 2

B2. You have read a newspaper article which says that international travel isn't worth the cost.

You have decided to write a letter to the newspaper to explain your point of view. You could write in favour or against international travel.

Write a letter to the newspaper giving your views.

> *Dear Sir or Madam,*
>
> *I read with dismay your recent article regarding international travel. As a regular traveller myself, I strongly disagree with your assertion that international travel is not worth the cost. The benefits of international travel far outweigh the expenses incurred: it broadens the mind, adds to your wealth of experience and heightens your awareness of the world around you.*
>
> *The article claims that UK holidays are cheaper and provide similar benefits. If you are not deterred by the threat of drizzle, perhaps that is true. To me, however, it is worth spending a fraction more to avoid wasting your holidays sheltering from the British rain.*

This letter is for somebody in a position of authority, so it uses a formal greeting.

Formal language like this helps to set the right tone for your letter and shows that you've understood your audience.

You need to make your viewpoint clear.

Introducing a counter-argument, then contradicting it, can help to build up your argument.

A love letter has a very specific purpose and audience...

...but you probably won't be asked to write one in the exam. You will need to pay attention to purpose and audience though. Make sure your letter completes the task in the question and is written in an appropriate style.

Sample Exam — Paper 1

These two pages show you some example questions that are like the ones you'll see in paper 1 — the source to go with questions A1-A5 is on pages 64-65. First have a good read through the questions and the source, then have a look at the handy graded answer extracts we've provided on pages 65-75.

Section A — Reading

Section A: 40 marks

Read carefully the passage on pages 64-65. Then answer all the questions below.

This question gives you a section of the text to look at. The facts that you use to answer the question must come from this part of the text.

A1. **Read lines 1-10.**

List **five** reasons why crossing the desert is difficult.

You just need to list the reasons (in short quotes or your own words). There's no need to write anything else about them.

You'll get one mark for each reason that you find.

[5 marks]

A2. **Read lines 11-17.**

How does the writer show the tribe's suffering?

Answers to this question need to focus specifically on the suffering that the tribe is enduring.

You must refer to the language used in the text to support your answer.

[5 marks]

For questions that ask 'how' the writer has done something, you need to write about the methods the writer has used and their effect on the reader.

In this case, you would need to focus on the effects of the writer's language on the reader, using quotes to support your answer.

A3. **Read lines 18-26.**

What impressions do you get of the men from these lines?

This question asks you to write about how the men are presented, but also how the text influences you as a reader.

You must refer to the text to support your answer.

[10 marks]

Make sure your answers include examples from the text to support your points.

A4. **Read lines 27-39.**

How does the writer make these lines mysterious?

This is another 'how' question — it asks you to write about the techniques the writer has used to make the text mysterious.

You should write about:

* the writer's use of language to create mystery;
* how the text's structure builds mystery;
* the effects on the reader.

Answers need to include examples of each of the things mentioned in the bullet points.

[10 marks]

Sample Exam — Paper 1

A5. **Read lines 40 to the end.**

This question is a bit different — it asks you to write about a specific part of the text and the text as a whole.

"In the last two paragraphs of this passage, the writer encourages the reader to feel sympathy for the tribe."

Evaluate the text by explaining how much you agree with the statement.

To what extent do you agree with this view?

You need to write about your own opinion of the text and the methods the writer has used to make you feel like this.

You should write about:

- your own impressions of the tribe and its surroundings, both here and in the passage as a whole;
- how the writer has created these impressions.

You must refer to the text to support your answer.

You should always include plenty of evidence from the text in your answers.

[10 marks]

Section B — Writing

You will need to write a piece of prose fiction for this question — so don't write a piece of poetry or a play.

Section B: 40 marks

In this section, you will be assessed for the quality of your **creative prose writing** skills.

24 marks are awarded for communication and organisation.
16 marks are awarded for vocabulary, sentence structure, spelling and punctuation.

You should aim to write about 450-600 words.

For writing questions, you get marks for how you write (i.e. the language and structure you use) and the accuracy of your writing (i.e. your spelling, punctuation and grammar).

You're given four options, but you only need to pick one of them.

Choose **one** of the following titles for your writing:

Either, (a) Taking a Chance

Or, (b) The Cabin

Or, (c) Write about a time when you were at a theme park

Or, (d) Write a story which begins:
"At the time, I didn't know it was the wrong decision…"

[40 marks]

All of my English skills seem to have deserted me...

Ha ha ha. Sigh. The good news is that you don't have to answer these questions yourself, because I've done it for you. Read on for some sample answers, which will give you an idea of what you need to write in your exam.

Literature Extract

Here's the text to go with the questions on pages 62-63. It's an extract from the opening of the novel *Desert,* by J.M.G. Le Clézio, which was published in 1980. The extract describes a tribe's journey across a desert.

They walked noiselessly in the sand, slowly, not watching where they were going. The wind blew relentlessly, the desert wind, hot in the daytime, cold at night. The sand swirled about them, between the legs of the camels, lashing the faces of the women, who pulled the blue veils down over their eyes. The young children ran about, the babies cried, rolled up in the blue cloth on their mothers' backs. The

5 camels growled, sneezed. No one knew where the caravan was going.

The sun was still high in the stark sky, sounds and smells were swept away on the wind. Sweat trickled slowly down the faces of the travelers; the dark skin on their cheeks, on their arms and legs was tinted with indigo. The blue tattoos on the women's foreheads looked like shiny little beetles. Their black eyes, like drops of molten metal, hardly seeing the immense stretch of sand, searched for signs of the trail in

10 the rolling dunes.

There was nothing else on earth, nothing, no one. They were born of the desert, they could follow no other path. They said nothing. Wanted nothing. The wind swept over them, through them, as if there were no one on the dunes. They had been walking since the very crack of dawn without stopping, thirst and weariness hung over them like a lead weight. Their cracked lips and tongues were

15 hard and leathery. Hunger gnawed their insides. They couldn't have spoken. They had been as mute as the desert for so long, filled with the light of the sun burning down in the middle of the empty sky, and frozen with the night and its still stars.

They continued to make their slow way down the slope toward the valley bottom, zigzagging when loose sand shifted out from under their feet. The men chose where their feet would come down without

20 looking. It was as if they were walking along invisible trails leading them out to the other end of solitude, to the night. Only one of them carried a gun, a flintlock rifle with a long barrel of blackened copper. He carried it on his chest, both arms folded tightly over it, the barrel pointing upward like a flagpole. His brothers walked alongside him, wrapped in their cloaks, bending slightly forward under the weight of their burdens. Beneath their cloaks, the blue clothing was in tatters, torn by thorns, worn by the sand.

25 Behind the weary herd, Nour, the son of the man with the rifle, walked in front of his mother and sisters. His face was dark, sun-scorched, but his eyes shone and the light of his gaze was almost supernatural.

They were the men and the women of the sand, of the wind, of the light, of the night. They had appeared as if in a dream at the top of a dune, as if they were born of the cloudless sky and carried the harshness of space in their limbs. They bore with them hunger, the thirst of bleeding lips, the flintlike

30 silence of the glinting sun, the cold nights, the glow of the Milky Way, the moon; accompanying them were their huge shadows at sunset, the waves of virgin sand over which their splayed feet trod, the inaccessible horizon. More than anything, they bore the light of their gaze shining so brightly in the whites of their eyes.

The herd of grayish-brown goats and sheep walked in front of the children. The beasts also moved

35 forward not knowing where, their hooves following in ancient tracks. The sand whirled between their legs, stuck in their dirty coats. One man led the dromedaries* simply with his voice, grumbling and spitting as they did. The hoarse sound of labored breathing caught in the wind, then suddenly disappeared in the hollows of the dunes to the south. But the wind, the dryness, the hunger, no longer mattered. The people and the herd moved slowly down toward the waterless, shadeless valley bottom.

40 They'd been walking like that for months, years maybe. They'd followed the routes of the sky between the waves of sand, the routes coming from the Drâa**, from Tamgrout, from the Erg Iguidi, or farther north — the route of the Aït Atta, of the Gheris, coming from Tafilelt, that joins the great *ksours*** in the foothills of the Atlas Mountains, or else the endless route that penetrates into the heart of the desert, beyond Hank, in the direction of the great city of Timbuktu. Some died along the way, others were born,

45 were married. Animals died too, throats slit open to fertilize the entrails of the earth, or else stricken with the plague and left to rot on the hard ground.

Graded Answer — Question A1

It was as if there were no names here, as if there were no words. The desert cleansed everything in its wind, wiped everything away. The men had the freedom of the open spaces in their eyes, their skin was like metal. Sunlight blazed everywhere. The ochre, yellow, gray, white sand, the fine sand
50 shifted, showing the direction of the wind. It covered all traces, all bones. It repelled light, drove away water, life, far from a center that no one could recognize. The men knew perfectly well that the desert wanted nothing to do with them: so they walked on without stopping, following the paths that other feet had already traveled in search of something else. As for water, it was in the *aiun*: the eyes that were the color of the sky, or else in the damp beds of old muddy streams. But it wasn't water for pleasure
55 or for refreshment either. It was just a sweat mark on the surface of the desert, the meager gift of an arid God, the last shudder of life. Heavy water wrenched from the sand, dead water from crevices, alkaline water that caused colic, vomiting. They must walk even farther, bending slightly forward, in the direction the stars had indicated.

Glossary
*   dromedaries — camels
**   Drâa, Tamgrout, Erg Iguidi, Aït Atta, Gheris, Tafilelt — places, regions and tribes of North Africa
*** *ksours* — fortified villages

Now that you've had a chance to look at the questions and the text, the next few pages have some sample answers for you to look at. This is a sample answer to question A1 on p.62.

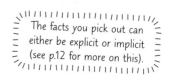

Better watch out for speed humps...

Check your facts carefully

1) Question A1 asks for <u>five</u> reasons why crossing the desert is difficult. You get <u>one</u> mark for <u>each</u> correct reason you write down.

2) There's no need to <u>analyse</u> the facts or add any extra information — the examiner is looking for your ability to <u>find</u> information from the text.

3) Careful though — <u>all</u> the facts need to come from <u>lines 1-10</u> of the text.

4) It's also important to <u>check</u> every fact carefully — anything that's <u>inaccurate</u> or doesn't refer to why crossing the desert is <u>difficult</u> won't get a mark.

5) You can lose marks if you use quotes that are too <u>long</u>, so don't just copy out <u>whole sentences</u> or huge <u>chunks</u> of text.

The facts you pick out can either be explicit or implicit (see p.12 for more on this).

You should be aiming for full marks on this question if you're after grades 8-9.

This is a grade 4-5 answer

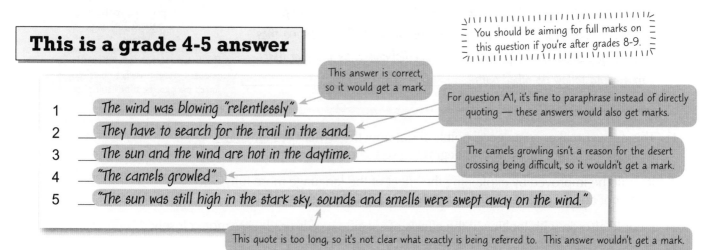

1 ___ The wind was blowing "relentlessly".
2 ___ They have to search for the trail in the sand.
3 ___ The sun and the wind are hot in the daytime.
4 ___ "The camels growled".
5 ___ "The sun was still high in the stark sky, sounds and smells were swept away on the wind."

This answer is correct, so it would get a mark.

For question A1, it's fine to paraphrase instead of directly quoting — these answers would also get marks.

The camels growling isn't a reason for the desert crossing being difficult, so it wouldn't get a mark.

This quote is too long, so it's not clear what exactly is being referred to. This answer wouldn't get a mark.

Graded Answers — Question A2

Question A2 (take a look back at p.62) is a tad trickier. Luckily, I've prepared some lovely sample answers...

Pick out key language features and explain their effects

1) Question A2 tests how well you can explain the <u>effects</u> of the <u>language</u> used in the extract.

2) The sample question asks you specifically about the language used to show the <u>tribe's suffering</u> — so you shouldn't write about the language used to describe <u>anything else</u>.

3) You need to include <u>technical terms</u> when you're describing the writer's techniques.

4) Every point you make should be backed up with an <u>example</u> that's fully <u>explained</u> and <u>developed</u> — you could use <u>P.E.E.D.</u> to help you with this (see p.4).

5) Here are some things you could <u>write</u> about:

- The effect of specific <u>words and phrases</u>, such as how specific verbs and adjectives are used (see p.27-28).

- <u>Language features and techniques</u>, such as metaphors, similes and personification (see p.29-32).

- The effect of different <u>sentence forms</u>, such as long or short sentences (see p.42-43).

Grant didn't need P.E.E.D. — he knew he could rely on his friends to back him up.

Here's a grade 4-5 answer extract

In the text it mentions that "Their cracked lips and tongues were hard and leathery. Hunger gnawed their insides. They couldn't have spoken". The fact that their lips and tongues are dry suggests that they don't have enough water, which makes you think they must be suffering.

The extract also uses a metaphor and a simile which says that their thirst and tiredness "hung over them like a lead weight". This makes their suffering sound like a burden, as lead weights are very heavy.

The tribe is described as being "born of the desert", suggesting they have a special relationship with it. This is emphasised by the fact that "they could follow no other path".

> It's great to include quotes, but try to keep them short.

> It's important to mention techniques like this, but you must always give an example and explain its effect.

> This analyses the effect of the simile and relates it to the tribe's suffering.

> This last paragraph isn't relevant to the question — it needs to be clearly linked back to the tribe's suffering.

1) This answer makes some good points about how the writer uses <u>language</u> to <u>show</u> the tribe's suffering and begins to use some <u>technical terms</u>.

2) It could be improved by <u>explaining</u> the <u>effect</u> of the language more fully, as it's not always <u>clear</u> how the examples are relevant to the <u>question</u>.

3) It could also do with looking at the effects of <u>specific words</u> or <u>phrases</u> more closely.

Graded Answers — Question A2

Here's a grade 6-7 answer extract

Referring to the writer shows that you understand they chose to use this language for a reason.

The writer says that the tribe's "cracked lips and tongues were hard and leathery". The fact that their lips are "cracked" demonstrates their thirst, but it also sounds painful, so it shows how much they are suffering. The writer also says that this thirst "hung over them like a lead weight". This simile suggests that thirst is a constant burden that the tribe cannot forget.

Imagery such as "Hunger gnawed their insides" highlights that the tribe's suffering is severe. The verb "gnawed" personifies the hunger, which makes it seem like it is deliberately trying to hurt the tribe. As a result, the tribe appears vulnerable, which makes their suffering seem inescapable.

Repetition also reflects the tribe's suffering. The repetition of "nothing" and "no one" in the first sentence helps the reader to understand that the tribe's suffering is partly emotional, caused by the isolation and emptiness of the surrounding desert.

It's great to use short, embedded quotes like this.

It's really good to focus on the effects of specific words.

It's important to keep linking the answer back to the question.

1) This answer makes some good points about the effects of the language the writer has chosen, which are backed up with appropriate quotations and linked back to the question.

2) It could be improved by analysing the language features and techniques in even more detail.

3) The final paragraph could also be more clear — it doesn't analyse how the repetition shows the tribe's emotional suffering.

This is a grade 8-9 answer extract

The answer uses a technical term correctly, and links its effect back to the question.

The tribe is objectified in the sentence that begins "The wind swept over them, through them", demonstrating that its people are at the mercy of the elements. This makes their suffering seem inevitable and makes the tribe appear vulnerable. This is emphasised by the personification of hunger, which "gnawed their insides". The verb "gnawed" is reminiscent of a predator consuming its prey, which helps the reader to visualise the pain and hardship that the tribe are facing and perceive them as helpless victims.

The writer also uses short, simple sentences to mirror the tribe's exhaustion, for example "They couldn't have spoken." and "They said nothing. Wanted nothing." The length of these sentences makes the text abrupt, and reminds the reader of the slow, heavy footsteps of the tribe, highlighting their exhaustion. The repetition of "they" in these sentences is also used throughout the rest of the paragraph; this keeps the reader's attention focused on the suffering of the tribe, suggesting its presence is constant.

It's important to focus on the effect of the language.

This answer uses a good range of short quotes to back up the points.

This answer stays focused on the question throughout.

1) This is a really good answer. It makes a range of perceptive points about the writer's choice of language and the effect it has, and then develops each point fully.

2) It also uses complex technical terms correctly and supports each point with relevant quotations.

Graded Answers — Question A3

Question A3 is the non-identical twin of question A2 — it's focused on language, but has its own personal twist. Don't worry — you're not expected to do extra work for nothing. There are 5 extra marks up for grabs.

Think about how language makes the reader feel

1) Question A3 (see p.62) is also about <u>language</u> and the <u>effects</u> it creates, but you're being asked to consider how language <u>influences the reader</u> as well.

2) This means you need to think about how the writer uses certain <u>words</u> or <u>techniques</u> to affect how the reader <u>feels</u> about the <u>men</u>.

3) Just like question A2, you could use <u>P.E.E.D.</u> to write your answer, and you need to use <u>technical terms</u> accurately.

4) You could <u>mention</u> some of these things:

Toby and Rover were unavailable to comment on how the text made them feel.

- The effects of <u>specific words and phrases</u>, such as how particular verbs are used (see p.27-28).

- The effects of different <u>language features</u> such as similes and alliteration (see p.29-32).

- The effects of different <u>sentence forms</u>, such as long or short sentences (see p.42-43).

- How these techniques influence the reader's <u>attitude</u> and <u>emotions</u>.

> Remember to always read the question carefully — it might only give you a specific part of the text to discuss.

Here's a grade 4-5 answer extract

In the passage, the writer uses alliteration when describing the men: "the blue clothing was in tatters, torn by thorns". The words "tatters" and "torn" stand out, showing the difficulties the men have faced during their journey. These words might also suggest that the men are poor.

The men seem experienced and skilled, as they "chose where their feet would come down without looking". This also makes it sound like they're sleepwalking, which might suggest that they're feeling very tired.

The writer describes the way the man holds the gun with "the barrel pointing upward like a flagpole", which makes the reader think that he might be the leader of the men. The text describes the other men as "brothers", which shows that they are close, so the reader feels curious about their relationship.

> This is good — the effects of specific words are explained.

> The paragraph begins with a clear point, which links back to the question.

> This point could be improved by explaining more clearly how the language influences the reader's attitude.

> This begins to analyse the impact of language on the reader, but it needs a clearer explanation.

1) This answer identifies some <u>language features</u> and describes some of their <u>effects</u>.

2) It could be improved by following the <u>P.E.E.D. structure</u> more closely — it needs to <u>explain</u> the effects in detail and <u>link</u> each point to the way the <u>men</u> are presented in the passage.

3) It also doesn't go into enough <u>detail</u> about how these features <u>influence</u> the reader.

Graded Answers — Question A3

Here's a grade 6-7 answer extract

The men appear unified in this passage. Despite the "weight of their burdens" they walk together, with one man holding a gun "like a flagpole". This simile implies that the men are united in a purpose, putting the reader in the mind of a march to war and creating a sense of intrigue, as the reader is left wondering what it is that they are marching towards.

The men are presented as accustomed to travelling the difficult route across the desert. The fact that they can follow "invisible trails", even though they can't see them, shows that they know the route well; this suggests to the reader that they have travelled in this direction many times before, as well as emphasising their skill at navigating the terrain.

The writer also makes the men seem weary. He describes how they are "bending slightly forward", which emphasises the physical hardships that they are enduring and suggests that they are being gradually beaten down by them. This shows that their journey has been long and difficult.

> This is a strong paragraph — it considers language, its effect and the impact this has on the reader.

> This explains the idea of the men being 'weary', but it doesn't go into enough detail about the effect this has on the reader.

1) This answer makes several good points about the <u>men</u>, and every point is <u>backed up</u> with <u>clearly-explained evidence</u> from the text.

2) The <u>effect</u> of the <u>language</u> on the <u>reader</u> is considered in places, but it doesn't do it <u>consistently</u> or in enough <u>detail</u>.

This is a grade 8-9 answer extract

The men are presented as fatigued and dishevelled, with their clothing "in tatters, torn by thorns". The alliterative 't' sounds create a harsh tone that emphasises the difficult reality of their lives; this encourages the reader to feel sympathy towards them. This feeling of sympathy is furthered by the men's evident vulnerability; the writer's assertion that "Only one of them carried a gun" implies that the tribe needs to protect itself, but only has limited means of doing so.

The writer also emphasises that the men's ability to cross the desert is deeply ingrained within them, as they "chose where their feet would come down without looking." The use of the verb "chose" to describe their actions emphasises the deliberateness with which they decide their path, and the fact that they are able to place their steps "without looking" suggests that they are familiar with the desert trails. This gives the reader the impression that, despite all the hardships they face, there is a certainty about their progress.

> Accurate use of technical terms makes the writing sound sophisticated.

> This develops a point about the way the language influences the reader's attitude towards the men.

> It's great to analyse specific words like this.

> This clearly links the point back to the question.

This is a <u>really good</u> answer — it makes <u>interesting</u> points about language and the way it affects the reader's impressions of the men. The points are <u>fully developed</u> and <u>technical terms</u> are used accurately.

Graded Answers — Question A4

Now you've got analysing language down to a fine art, you should be ready to tackle question A4.
This question is about the effects of structure, as well as language. (So demanding, I know.)

Link your points back to the effect on the reader

1) Question A4 on p.62 asks about how the writer uses <u>language</u> and <u>structure</u> to make lines 27-39 of the text <u>mysterious</u>.

2) When answering this question, you need to include <u>technical terms</u>, and you should use <u>P.E.E.D.</u>

Remember — structure is how a writer has organised their ideas in a text.

3) To get top marks, you need to write about <u>everything</u> the bullet points mention:

> - How <u>language features</u> and <u>specific words</u> (see p.27-32) create a sense of <u>mystery</u> in the passage.
>
> - How the <u>structure</u> (see p.40-41) of the text makes it seem more <u>mysterious</u>.
>
> - You also need to write about how these techniques influence the reader's <u>attitude</u> and <u>emotions</u>.

Kim had found an easy way to make her new book seem mysterious.

© ayzek/iStockphoto.com

Here's a grade 4-5 answer extract

> The writer creates a sense of mystery because it isn't clear why the tribe are travelling. The valley they are heading towards is described as "waterless, shadeless", but the tribe seem to be heading in that direction. This makes the tribe seem mysterious and confusing, as the reader doesn't understand why they have decided to make such an apparently illogical decision.
>
> Repetition is used to describe the tribe as "of the sand, of the wind, of the light, of the night". This makes it seem like the tribe are a part of nature.
>
> The image of the men and women appearing "as if in a dream at the top of a dune" uses alliteration, which makes the words stand out from the rest of the text. This emphasises that the tribe seem dream-like — it's as if they are not real, which makes the text even more mysterious.

The paragraph begins by linking the point back to the question.

It's important to mention the effect on the reader, but this could go into a bit more detail about how the language creates this effect.

This paragraph mentions the effect of a structural feature, but it doesn't clearly explain how it makes this part of the text mysterious.

1) This answer discusses both <u>structure</u> and <u>language</u>, and starts to consider their <u>effects</u>.

2) However, it doesn't go into enough <u>detail</u> — it needs to explain more clearly how the <u>writer's techniques</u> create these effects.

3) It also needs to focus more on the <u>topic</u> in the question — not all the points are clearly linked to why the text feels <u>mysterious</u>.

Graded Answers — Question A4

This is a grade 6-7 answer extract

There is a contrast between the fifth and sixth paragraphs of the text. The fifth paragraph uses figurative language to describe the tribe and their journey, comparing the desert to the "waves" of the sea and referring to the "glow of the Milky Way". In the sixth paragraph, however, the focus is on more everyday topics, such as the "grayish-brown goats and sheep". This focus on small, mundane elements of the tribespeople's lives helps to emphasise the mystery of the previous paragraph by providing a contrast for the reader.

This sense of mystery in the extract is emphasised by the writer's description of the desert. Its "inaccessible horizon" makes it sound vast and complex. This is combined with the mention of "ancient tracks", which hints at the desert's long history. The writer uses these phrases to emphasise how little the reader knows about the desert, which increases the sense of mystery that surrounds it.

This makes a clear point about structure and links its effects back to the question.

Good use of a brief quote to back up a point.

The points in this answer are clearly linked back to the question.

1) This answer explores how a sense of <u>mystery</u> is created in the passage, looking at the effects of both <u>language</u> and <u>structure</u>. Each paragraph <u>links</u> back to the question.

2) It could be improved by <u>analysing</u> the writer's techniques in even more <u>detail</u>.

Here's a grade 8-9 answer extract

The writer creates a sense of mystery through the use of imagery, linking the tribe to huge concepts such as nature, heaven and space. The tribe were born directly "of the cloudless sky", linking them to gods and the heavens; they were the people "of the sand, of the wind, of the light", which links the tribe to all of nature; finally, they carried with them "the glow of the Milky Way, the moon", which broadens their link to the greater universe and makes them seem almost ethereal. These images create a dramatic sense of mystery by making the tribe seem so much more than mere people, which in turn makes the reader question their presence.

This feeling of unreality is emphasised by the writer's complex use of sentence construction in the long sentence on lines 29-32. This introduces a series of images in quick succession, which mimics the uneven pace and illogical sequence of dreams, and creates a complex mosaic of images for the reader. This adds to the sense of mystery in the passage by making the text feel less rooted in real life, as the reader experiences the dreamlike sequencing of the description.

This answer looks at the specific effects of lots of parts of the language, and links them all back to the question.

The effect on the reader is covered for each point.

More complex vocabulary makes this answer stand out.

1) This answer makes perceptive points about both <u>structure</u> and <u>language</u>, and their <u>effects</u>.

2) It goes into lots of <u>detail</u> and uses technical terms <u>accurately</u>.

Graded Answers — Question A5

Question A5 (see p.63) is worth another 10 marks, and is the last question in Section A.
Here are some helpful ideas on how you would go about answering it...

Write about whether you agree with the statement and why

1) This question asks you to <u>evaluate</u> the text by saying how much you <u>agree</u> with the statement.

2) This means you need to explain <u>how much</u> the lines make the reader feel <u>sympathy</u> for the tribe, and <u>how</u> the writer achieves this.

3) You need to <u>back up</u> your opinion using evidence from the text, and <u>explain</u> and <u>develop</u> your points clearly (use <u>P.E.E.D.</u>).

4) The bullet points under the question give you guidance about what you <u>need</u> to include in your answer:

Timmy always found enough evidence when evaluating a text.

- You need to write about <u>your own feelings</u> as you read the text — whether or not you <u>feel sympathy</u> for the tribe.

- You also need to write about the <u>techniques</u> the writer uses to create these feelings, i.e. the <u>language</u> or <u>structural devices</u> they use.

- You should <u>focus</u> on the lines that the question specifies, but you should mention <u>other parts</u> of the passage to support your answer.

Here's a grade 4-5 answer extract

> I think that the statement is true: the reader is encouraged to feel sympathy for the tribe. The narrator isn't clear about how long the tribe have been travelling: "months, years maybe". This makes it seem like they have been travelling for too long to remember accurately, and have had a hard life, so I feel sorry for them.
>
> The reader feels sorry for the tribe because their life is clearly very tough, partly because of the heat. The writer talks about how the sunlight "blazed" on line 49, and elsewhere in the passage it is also described as "burning". The reader gets the sense that the tribe's environment is unfriendly and dangerous.
>
> The image of the animals with their "throats slit open" and "left to rot" makes the reader feel sympathetic because it is disgusting. The fact that this has happened increases the reader's sympathy for the trials the tribe have gone through.

This is good — it gives an opinion on the statement.

Mentioning other parts of the passage shows that you're thinking about the text as a whole.

This hasn't explained how the words 'blazed' and 'burning' make the tribe's environment seem dangerous.

This mentions the effect on the reader, but doesn't clearly explain how the text creates this effect.

1) This answer starts to <u>comment</u> on the difficulties the tribe have gone through, and how this makes the <u>reader</u> feel sympathy for them.

2) However, some of the points in this answer need to be <u>developed</u> further by explaining <u>how</u> the writer's choice of language and structure <u>affects</u> the reader.

Graded Answers — Question A5

Here's a grade 6-7 answer extract

I strongly agree that the writer of the text creates sympathy for the travellers. It is made clear that the tribe have no choice but to continue on their difficult journey when the writer explains that the tribe "must walk even farther". The word "must" emphasises that this is a necessity rather than a choice; this makes the reader feel sympathy for the tribe because they seem forced to endure difficult conditions, with no way to avoid them.

The difficulty of their lives is emphasised by the use of a long sentence on lines 40-44, in which the narrator lists a series of routes they've followed. The length of this sentence mirrors the length of the tribe's journey, and the list of places, tribes and regions creates a relentless tone that suggests the tribe haven't been able to properly rest or stop for a long time. This increases the reader's sympathy by emphasising the prolonged difficulties that the tribe have had to face.

> This shows that you've thought about the extent to which you agree with the statement.

> This answer picks out specific words and comments on their impact.

> This clearly explains the effect that the language creates.

1) This answer clearly focuses on how the writer creates sympathy for the tribe.

2) It uses a good range of relevant quotes as evidence, and develops the points by relating them to the effect on the reader.

This is a grade 8-9 answer extract

The writer is highly successful in creating sympathy for the tribe. This is achieved by emphasising the harsh environment of the desert. For example, he uses a metaphor, describing the available water as a "sweat mark on the surface of the desert", which had to be "wrenched from the sand". By comparing water to "sweat", the writer links finding water to hard work; this impression is reinforced by the verb "wrenched", which implies hard effort and powerful movements. By focusing on something that many people take for granted, and illustrating how difficult it is for the tribespeople to acquire it, the writer clearly emphasises the difficulties of desert life; this may invoke the reader's sympathy because it contrasts with their own life experiences.

The harsh desert environment is also emphasised by the reference to "the meager gift of an arid God" on lines 55-56. The adjective "meager" makes the reader feel sympathy for the tribe, as it suggests that they are forced to survive on limited resources. The subsequent reference to the water as the "gift" of a god is used ironically, as that gift will cause illnesses such as "colic, vomiting". This makes the reader feel even more sympathy for the tribe, because it suggests that even their god cannot or will not help them.

> This answer gives a clear response to the statement, then goes on to explain how the writer achieves this effect.

> This shows an understanding of how the text's language affects the reader's response.

> This analyses the language used in the extract in detail.

> Keep referring back to the statement to make sure your answer is focused.

This is a top grade answer — it clearly responds to the statement in an original way, and its points are backed up with relevant quotes and examples.

Graded Answers — Section B

Section B is your chance to get creative. You'll have a choice of four tasks — go for whichever one you feel most inspired by, but don't waste too much time deciding. See p.63 for the full question.

Your writing needs to interest the reader

1) The purpose of creative writing is always to entertain the reader. You need to use a range of sophisticated vocabulary and language techniques that will be interesting for the reader.

2) Your writing has to have an interesting plot and characters. To get top marks, these need to be original and well-developed.

3) Your writing also needs to be really descriptive — make sure you describe the scene and the characters in an interesting and detailed way.

4) The structure of your writing is really important. You need to write in a way that is intriguing to the reader and keeps them gripped throughout your story.

5) There are loads of marks on offer for spelling, punctuation and grammar in this question, so it's really important to write accurately (see pages 10-11).

Roy suspected his attempt to interest Clara was failing rather badly.

Here's a grade 4-5 answer extract

All these extracts are from answers to the second title ('The Cabin') listed in the sample question on p.63.

> The small house stood on its own, surrounded by fir trees and rocks. Snow had gathered against the walls in deep piles. It did not look very inviting, but to Anneka it was the most welcome sight in the world. She had got lost in the woods and she had been worried that she would have to spend the night outside in the forest, which was freezing cold and as scary as a spider's nest.
>
> Anneka walked towards the door and knocked. To her surprise the door swung open and she could see inside the house. She saw a single room with a fire burning in the fireplace and a table set for two, with hot food piled high on the plates. There was only one thing missing from the scene, there were no people inside.
>
> Anneka walked tentatively into the room and began to warm her hands in front of the fire, wondering where the people who lived in the house had gone. The room looked as if someone had just stepped out, but the only path Anneka had seen was the one she had come along, and she had not passed anyone else. Surely they couldn't have just disappeared?

This sets the scene, but it could do with some more imaginative description.

It's good to use descriptive techniques like similes, but this one isn't very original and it doesn't really create the right tone.

The punctuation in this sentence isn't quite right — a colon would fit better.

This is a good piece of descriptive vocabulary.

This sets up a mystery, which makes the reader want to know what has happened.

1) This answer has a fairly clear structure and gets straight into the story.

2) However, it lacks description, and the vocabulary isn't very varied. It could also be made more exciting or complex to make it more entertaining.

3) The character in the story could be developed further to give the reader a better sense of her personality or appearance.

Graded Answers — Section B

Here's a grade 6-7 answer extract

Robin lowered the axe he had been using to chop wood and peered towards the mountains, his eyes squinting in the sharp orange glow of the slowly setting Sun. He was sure he had seen a movement up there, a flash of scarlet against the sparkling white of the snow-capped peaks. But who would be mad enough to venture into the mountains at dusk, in winter, with snow and freezing temperatures forecast that night?

Robin sighed wearily, deciding that it must have been his imagination playing tricks on him, as it so often did out here in the mountains.

A low, ominous rumble echoed down the valley, interrupting his thoughts. Robin froze momentarily, listening intently, then snapped into action, frantically gathering his tools as the sound grew louder and closer.

The avalanche roared destructively and unstoppably towards his isolated home.

This uses the opening sentence of the story to set the scene nicely.

This answer uses interesting language to make the descriptions more vivid and to entertain the reader.

This uses the senses to help the reader to imagine the scene.

The change of pace creates excitement in this story.

1) This has a clear <u>structure</u>, uses good <u>descriptions</u> and builds <u>interest</u> for the reader.

2) It could be improved by using more <u>complex</u> sentence structures and a <u>wider range</u> of punctuation.

This is a grade 8-9 answer extract

I surfaced suddenly from a dreamless sleep, the skin on my forearms tingling with an instinctive awareness that something was wrong. There — that noise again! A skittering, scrabbling, scuffling noise in the far corner of the dimly lit room. I sat up in bed, the quilt clutched to my chest with stone-numb hands, my breath forming foggy billows in the chilly air.

The sun was just rising; its feeble light trickled through the window, fractured into myriad rainbows by the intricate whorls and fingers of ice on the frosty pane. As a brighter beam pierced the gloom, I gasped. There, huddled by the door, a young wolf cub gazed at me with sorrowful, strangely human eyes. His tawny fur was matted with blood, as rich and red as the morning light that now illuminated it fully.

I eased myself out of the wooden bunk, crouched down on the splintered floorboards and held out a trembling hand towards the cub. He gazed at me uncertainly, then slowly, slowly, he stretched forward and snuffled at my fingers, his breath as warm and ticklish as a damp feather duster.

This beginning immediately sets the tone and atmosphere by creating tension.

This uses a first-person narrator to establish a strong connection with the reader.

Vivid description and interesting vocabulary help to set the scene.

Unusual imagery helps to set this answer apart.

1) This has a structure that <u>interests</u> the reader by <u>slowly revealing</u> what's going on.

2) It's also packed with imaginative <u>imagery</u> and unusual <u>vocabulary</u> to make it more <u>entertaining</u> to read, which helps it to fit the <u>purpose</u> of the question.

Sample Exam — Paper 2

These two pages show you some example questions that are like the ones you'll see in paper 2 — the texts to go with questions A1-A6 are on pages 78-79. First have a good read through the questions and the texts, then have a look at the handy graded answer extracts we've provided on pages 80-93.

Section A — Reading

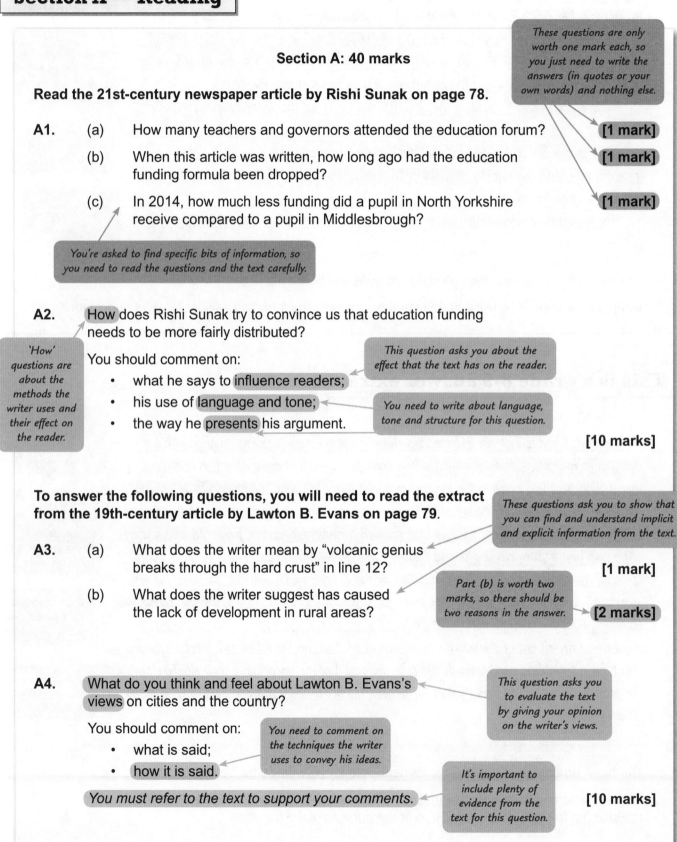

Section A: 40 marks

Read the 21st-century newspaper article by Rishi Sunak on page 78.

These questions are only worth one mark each, so you just need to write the answers (in quotes or your own words) and nothing else.

A1. (a) How many teachers and governors attended the education forum? **[1 mark]**

(b) When this article was written, how long ago had the education funding formula been dropped? **[1 mark]**

(c) In 2014, how much less funding did a pupil in North Yorkshire receive compared to a pupil in Middlesbrough? **[1 mark]**

You're asked to find specific bits of information, so you need to read the questions and the text carefully.

A2. How does Rishi Sunak try to convince us that education funding needs to be more fairly distributed?

'How' questions are about the methods the writer uses and their effect on the reader.

You should comment on:

This question asks you about the effect that the text has on the reader.

• what he says to influence readers;

• his use of language and tone;

You need to write about language, tone and structure for this question.

• the way he presents his argument.

[10 marks]

To answer the following questions, you will need to read the extract from the 19th-century article by Lawton B. Evans on page 79.

These questions ask you to show that you can find and understand implicit and explicit information from the text.

A3. (a) What does the writer mean by "volcanic genius breaks through the hard crust" in line 12? **[1 mark]**

(b) What does the writer suggest has caused the lack of development in rural areas?

Part (b) is worth two marks, so there should be two reasons in the answer.

[2 marks]

A4. What do you think and feel about Lawton B. Evans's views on cities and the country?

This question asks you to evaluate the text by giving your opinion on the writer's views.

You should comment on:

You need to comment on the techniques the writer uses to convey his ideas.

• what is said;

• how it is said.

You must refer to the text to support your comments.

It's important to include plenty of evidence from the text for this question.

[10 marks]

Sample Exam — Paper 2

To answer the following questions you will need to use both texts.

You need to write a summary — a piece of writing that combines ideas from both texts, but is written using your own words.

A5. According to these two writers, why does education in rural areas need to be focused on? **[4 marks]**

A6. Both of these texts are about education. Compare the following:

You need to write about how the writers use language and structure to achieve effects.

- the writers' attitudes to education;
- how they get across their arguments.

You must use the text to support your comments and make it clear which text you are referring to.

This question asks you to compare, so you need to write about how the writers' viewpoints are similar or different.

[10 marks]

Section B — Writing

This section requires you to answer both writing questions.

Section B: 40 marks

In this section, you will be assessed for the quality of your writing skills.

For each question, 12 marks are awarded for communication and organisation; 8 marks are awarded for vocabulary, sentence structure, punctuation and spelling.

You should aim to write about 300-400 words for each task.

For writing questions, you get marks for how you write (i.e. language and structure) and the accuracy of your writing (i.e. your spelling, punctuation and grammar).

B1. Your school wants to encourage students to take up more outdoor hobbies.

Your answer needs to incorporate both of these bullet points.

Write a report for the school governors suggesting ways this might be done.

You could include:

This question tells you the form (a report) and the audience (the school governors).

- examples of hobbies that students might enjoy;
- ideas for persuading students to take them up.

[20 marks]

B2. Your local council wants to encourage young people to have part-time jobs before the age of sixteen.

You are going to write an article for a broadsheet newspaper to share your views on this idea. You could agree or disagree with the council's idea.

Write an engaging article for a broadsheet newspaper giving your views. **[20 marks]**

You need to write a newspaper article for this question, but it asks you to give your opinion — so it needs to be written like a commentary rather than a news report (see p.53).

This time we've done the hard work for you...

It's a tricky ol' exam and no mistake. Just this once though, we've done it for you. Have a good look through the sources on pages 78-79 and our graded answers that follow, and you'll be more than a match for it.

21st-Century Source

Here are the exam sources to go with the questions on pages 76-77. On this page is a newspaper article written by an MP (Member of Parliament) called Rishi Sunak, which was published in October 2015.

Rishi Sunak: Why rural schools must receive a fairer deal on funding

ONE of my constituents summed it up best. Their belief was that education is the greatest single tool to allow you to change your own life and make an impact in your community.

5   My grandparents grew up on the other side of the world with very little. Two generations later, I have the incredible privilege of being a Member of Parliament. Many of us can tell similar stories of where our families started, what they worked to achieve and how their
10   efforts passed something on to the next generation. I am confident that all these journeys are built on the foundation of a strong education.

However, since becoming a Member of Parliament, it has become clear to me that our current means of distributing funding between schools is, at best, out of date and, at worst, unfair for our rural schools and local children.

15   This week I hosted an education forum with more than 50 local primary school teachers and governors to learn about their experiences. We agreed to work together and launch a campaign to fight for a better deal.

Many of our children and grandchildren attend wonderful village primary schools that are the beating hearts of their communities. But because of the nature of our countryside and the distances between
20   settlements, these schools will often be small.

There are particular costs of providing education in small rural settings that are often not well understood by policy-makers sitting in Whitehall. For example, it is often difficult to organise seven primary school year groups into a standard class structure and sometimes an additional half class is needed. More obviously, small schools cannot spread the cost of administration or leadership over a
25   large number of pupils.

The way funding was allocated between schools historically did not adequately recognise these factors. This led to significant problems in under-funded areas, in particular the East Riding* a decade ago, where there was talk of four-day weeks and mass redundancies.

Although people often talk about problems with the education funding formula, the reality is that
30   there is no formula. In response to crises like the one in East Riding, it was dropped a decade ago and, instead, whatever a local authority received then has been either uniformly increased or decreased.

So if your local area was under-funded 10 years ago, it will continue to be. If your local schools got a raw deal back then, they most likely still will do now. What was a temporary fix is now long overdue for reform.

35   Today two children, both on free school meals but living in different places, can receive very different sums of money for their education. Schools around the country that are similar can get very different budgets and children with the same needs can receive very different levels of financial support.

Last year, a pupil in my constituency in North Yorkshire received £500 less than a pupil only a few miles away in Middlesbrough. In the case of a city such as Manchester, the gap is as high as £700. A
40   pupil in one of the top five funded areas received over £2,000 more than North Yorkshire does.

This simply needs to change. In a climate where money is tight as we balance the books, it is even more important that schools receive their fair share.

At the forum I heard inspiring stories of what heads, teachers and governors are doing to ensure our local schools can continue to thrive. They all deserve their fair share of funding so they can continue to
45   do the vital job they do so well.

Providing a fairly funded and excellent education is one of this generation's most important responsibilities to undertake for the benefit of the next generation. We simply must get it right.

Glossary
* East Riding — a part of the county of Yorkshire in the north of England

19th-Century Source

This is the second exam source, which is an extract from an article published in a journal in 1896. It was written by Lawton B. Evans, an American teacher and educational leader.

THE COUNTY UNIT IN EDUCATIONAL ORGANIZATION

By Lawton B. Evans, Superintendent of Schools, Augusta, Ga.

The educational thought of our time has been chiefly directed toward the improvement of city school systems. So we hear of the great schools at Boston, Chicago, New York, Cincinnati, Philadelphia, and a score of other places; but I have yet to hear of a single county or township of rural population, the excellence of whose schools entitles them to national repute. The emphasis of our thought has been
5 placed long and devotedly on city schools at the expense of the rural schools.

It is true that cities are the centers of highest civilization. Our human nature has made them so. Architecture, art, literature, schools, fashion, reach their highest forms when people strive with each other for display. The very contact of people civilizes them. Cities are likewise the centers of greatest iniquity*. The worthless, the idle, the contentious, the wicked, gravitate toward large centers. Extremes of virtue
10 and vice meet. The force of cities attracts everything, good and bad alike. But cities do not develop individuality. There is a leveling influence about them that merges individuals into masses, and it is only occasionally that a volcanic genius breaks through the hard crust and thrusts itself above the burning level of great city life. The highest types of individuality, the strong and independent men of our nation, have been born and bred in village or rural homes, away from the turmoil of city life, in quiet and serious
15 communion with nature, in her grand and ennobling forms. It is out of the rural homes that the great men of our country have come. Genius abhors the palace and the crowded cities and the cradles of luxury, and courts the cabins and the open fields and the simple but stern homes of the poor.

We need skilled labor in the fields as well as in the city. We need intelligent and scientific management of a farm as well as of a great factory. We need business methods here as well as in
20 the great commercial houses of the city. We need economy of effort and conservation of force and adaptation of invention and discovery here, if we need it anywhere. And we need culture and refinement among the country people. Music, painting, books, and all the evidences of a higher kind of life are as proper on the farms as in the cities. The more highly educated the people of the rural districts are, the more capable they will be of taking advantage of the improvement in machinery, of economizing time and
25 labor in producing raw material, and the more time they will have to devote to culture and the higher arts of civilization. They will accomplish as much as now in far less time, and will live more comfortably and more happily.

That farm life is behind city life in development is due in some part to the isolation of the rural population. Men live too far apart and see each other too seldom to exert a refining influence over each
30 other. In other part, it is due to the attention that has been given to educating the people of the city.

It is quite time that we change the emphasis of our study, turn aside from the contemplation of the excellences of the city schools, and consider the necessities of the rural schools. The wisest policy is to frame some educational scheme that will keep the people in the country, that will stop the exodus from the farms, that will make the rural population content, that will make them enlightened and prosperous.

Glossary
* iniquity — sin

Graded Answers — Question A1

Not too much to write for question A1, you'll be pleased to hear.
Remind yourself of the question on p.76, then get stuck into this stuff to see how it's done.

Question A1 is in three parts

1) Question A1 asks you to answer <u>three</u> short questions about
   the <u>first text</u> — the newspaper article by Rishi Sunak.

2) This question is testing the ability to <u>find information and ideas</u> in the text.

3) There's <u>one</u> mark available for each part of the question, so you just need to write
   down <u>one fact</u>. There's no need to <u>analyse</u> the facts or give any <u>extra information</u>.

4) The questions ask you to find facts from <u>any part</u> of the text, so you need
   to read the whole text <u>thoroughly</u> to find the right information.

Here's a grade 4-5 answer

Part (a) has been answered <u>correctly</u> here, but (b) and (c)
are <u>wrong</u>, so this answer would only get <u>one</u> mark.

(a) over 50

(b) four days

(c) £700

> For question 1, it's fine to paraphrase instead of directly
> quoting — this answer would get a mark.

> These figures are both mentioned in the text, but they're not
> the right answers. Make sure you read the text and questions
> carefully so that you don't make any mistakes like this.

This is a grade 6-7 answer

Parts (a) and (b) have been answered <u>correctly</u> here, but
part (c) is <u>wrong</u>. This answer would get <u>two</u> marks.

(a) more than 50

(b) ten years

(c) £5000

> This has been written down
> incorrectly. Double-check your
> answers to avoid losing marks.

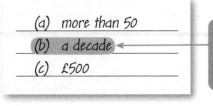

> Lisa's new job as a rural
> teacher wasn't quite
> what she'd expected.

And here's a grade 8-9 answer

This answer has got parts (a), (b) <u>and</u> (c)
correct, so it gets <u>three</u> marks.

(a) more than 50

(b) a decade

(c) £500

> 'Decade' and 'ten years' mean
> the same thing, and the text
> uses both phrases, so this
> answer would get a mark.

Section Six — Paper 2: Sample Exam and Graded Answers

Graded Answers — Question A2

It's time for question A2 (take a look back at p.76). Better get your thinking cap on...

Question A2 is about how the writer influences the reader

1) Question A2 asks you about <u>how</u> the writer achieves their <u>purpose</u> — to <u>persuade</u> the reader to agree with their point of view.

2) This means you need to comment on the writer's <u>techniques</u>, and explain the <u>effect</u> that they have on the reader.

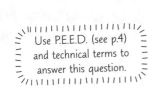
Use P.E.E.D. (see p.4) and technical terms to answer this question.

3) To do this, you need to write about <u>each</u> of the things mentioned in the <u>bullet points</u>. For this question, you would have to:

> • Write about the <u>points</u> Rishi Sunak makes in order to <u>persuade</u> the reader to agree with his point of view.
>
> • Explain how <u>language techniques</u> (see p.26-35) are used in the text to <u>persuade</u> the reader.
>
> • Write about the <u>tone</u> of the text (see p.25) and how it <u>persuades</u> the reader.
>
> • Explain how the <u>structure</u> of the text (see p.39) helps to <u>persuade</u> the reader.

4) You also need to include <u>quotes</u> and <u>examples</u> from the text to back up each point that you make.

This is a grade 4-5 answer extract

> The reader wants to agree with Rishi Sunak because he says he is a "Member of Parliament", which suggests that he is an expert in understanding political matters. This makes the reader more easily persuaded by anything that he says because they think they should trust his opinion.
>
> The writer also uses words like "obviously" and "simply" to make it seem like everybody should agree with him. This makes the reader trust the writer even more and agree that the government needs to change the way that schools receive money, especially in rural areas like North Yorkshire that get a "raw deal".
>
> The article has a conclusion that sums up the argument: the writer says that "fairly funded and excellent" education is an "important" responsibility, so the reader will clearly remember the writer's main argument.

This comments on the effect that the text has on the reader.

The way this bit is written is too long-winded, and needs to be more focused on the question.

It needs to be more clearly explained how the conclusion helps to make the article more persuasive.

1) This answer makes some points about <u>how</u> the writer <u>convinces</u> the reader to agree with his point of view.

2) However, some of the examples need to be <u>explained</u> more clearly and in more detail.

3) This answer could also be improved by including more <u>technical terms</u>.

Graded Answers — Question A2

Here's a grade 6-7 answer extract

The writer of the newspaper article uses several real-life examples to illustrate his point that rural schools are currently underfunded. These give the text a trustworthy, factual tone that makes the reader more likely to agree with the writer's argument. This is reinforced by his inclusion of statistics: the idea that some pupils receive "over £2,000 more" than others demonstrates that the way schools are funded currently is unfair, which makes the reader think it needs to be changed. The numbers also shock the reader, which might further persuade them to agree with Sunak's argument.

The structure of the article also helps to convince the reader to agree with Sunak's argument. For example, the extract ends with a short, simple sentence: "We simply must get it right." This has a powerful impact on the reader, because it adds to the reader's impression that Sunak's argument is uncomplicated: it is "simply" the right thing to do to change the way that educational funding is distributed.

> This is good — it starts with a clear point, then discusses the effect on the reader.

> This point has been really well developed by linking together different examples and their effects.

> For this question, it's important to comment on language **and** structure.

1) This answer clearly analyses the <u>effect</u> that the text has on the reader.

2) It could be improved by analysing the writer's use of <u>language</u> in more <u>detail</u>.

Here's a grade 8-9 answer extract

Rishi Sunak's article is structured so that it persuades the reader. It begins by using a short, emphatic first paragraph, which is used to immediately establish the key idea that education is the "greatest single tool" at our disposal. The superlative "greatest" shows the importance that Sunak places on education, and the fact that the idea is paraphrased from a "constituent" indicates that other people agree with Sunak's beliefs; this makes the reader more likely to be convinced by his argument.

After establishing the importance of education, Sunak then goes on to explain how a lack of funding is putting some children's education at risk. To illustrate this, he balances shocking statistics, such as the "£2,000" funding gap between children in different constituencies, with authoritative statements such as "This simply needs to change." These elements combine to create a confident, assured tone that helps to persuade the reader that Sunak's argument is justified.

Sunak also tries to persuade the reader using direct address, which is reinforced by the use of a repetitive sentence structure. The repetition of "If your local area" and "If your local schools" continually places emphasis on the word "your", which persuades the reader by suggesting that they could be individually affected by unfair funding.

> This is great — the effects of specific vocabulary choices are analysed in detail.

> It's important to link your answers back to the question.

> It's great to comment on the tone of a text as part of your analysis.

> This answer consistently refers back to the effect that the text has on the reader.

This answer makes a range of <u>well-developed</u> and <u>perceptive</u> points that clearly <u>answer the question</u>.

Graded Answers — Question A3

Question A3 is another fairly short question — it asks you to pick out a few key details from the 19th-century text. Take a look back at page p.76 to remind you of the question, then read the answers below.

You need to choose information carefully

1) Question A3 asks you to answer two short questions about the journal article by Lawton B. Evans.

2) It's testing the ability to find and understand information and ideas in the text.

3) For part (a) you just need to explain what the phrase means, with no extra analysis.

4) Part (b) is worth two marks, so the answer should give two reasons. There's no need to analyse the reasons or give any extra information.

5) You need to read the questions carefully, as they might be about something that is implicit — information that isn't stated outright, but is implied by what the text says.

Here's a grade 4-5 answer

Part (a) has been answered incorrectly here, and there's only one correct answer given for part (b). This answer would get one mark.

(a) It's a metaphor.

This answer doesn't explain what the phrase means, so it doesn't get a mark.

(b) Rural populations are very isolated.

Part (b) is worth two marks, so you need to pick out two details from the text. This answer is only worth one mark.

This is a grade 6-7 answer

Part (a) has been answered correctly here, but there's only one correct answer given for part (b), so it would only get two marks in total.

(a) Someone exceptional rises above everybody else.

(b) Men live too close together.

This isn't right, so it wouldn't get a mark.

Too much attention has been given to educating people in the cities.

It's fine to paraphrase or quote from the text, as long as the answer is accurate.

And here's a grade 8-9 answer

This answer has the correct responses for parts (a) and (b) — it gets full marks.

(a) Someone special rises above the "leveling" influence of the cities.

(b) People who live in rural areas are isolated from each other.

Too much attention has been given to educating people in the cities.

You only need to give two reasons to get full marks, even if there are more in the text.

Graded Answers — Question A4

Verily, in thy quest to slay the examination thou hast reached the fourth question. Journey to page p.76 to reacquaint thyself with thine enemy, then unsheathe thy biro and scream "En garde!" at question A4.

Think about the writer's choice of words

1) Question A4 is about your personal response to the writer's viewpoint. You need to evaluate the text by explaining your thoughts and feelings about the topic in the question.

2) For every point you make about what the writer has said, you also need to explain how the writer has used language and structure to convey their views.

3) The question reminds you to refer to the text in your answers, so you also need to use plenty of evidence from the text to back up each point.

4) To write a really good answer to this question, you need to show that you've engaged with the text — you need to express a detailed, clear understanding of the writer's viewpoint.

5) You should use the P.E.E.D. structure to write your answer to this question (see p.4 for more about this).

> Your evidence can either be paraphrased or quoted directly from the text — see page 5 for more about this.

Here's a grade 4-5 answer extract

I think that Lawton B. Evans is too harsh on cities. He thinks that "genius" can't emerge as easily in a city, and that some of the people there are "worthless" and "idle". This seems unfair. He does say some nice things about cities: they are full of "civilization", but he quickly moves on to the negative aspects of the city so I feel like, overall, the city is a bad place to be. In contrast, Evans is very nice about the countryside. He says that some men born in the countryside are "strong and independent", and thinks that they deserve "culture and refinement" just like the cities have. He says that their homes are "simple" and "stern" though, which makes the countryside seem like a bad place to live. Overall I think I prefer Evans's description of the countryside to the city, because it seems a lot more relaxing than the "Extremes of virtue and vice" that you see in cities.

Here, it needs to be explained how the text has this effect on the reader.

This linking sentence makes it clear that you're thinking about the writer's views on cities and the country.

This answer doesn't show a clear understanding of the writer's views and their purpose. The text wasn't about how relaxing cities and the countryside are — it was about why the countryside should receive more attention.

1) This starts to answer the question — it gives an evaluation of the text by commenting on how the reader thinks and feels about the writer's views.

2) Both the city and the countryside are commented on, and relevant examples are included to support the points being made.

3) There's room for improvement though — it needs to be explained how the writer's techniques have particular effects on the reader.

4) It would also be better to use more effective and sophisticated vocabulary, e.g. 'positive' instead of 'nice'.

Graded Answers — Question A4

Here's a grade 6-7 answer extract

Evans presents a view of cities that is a combination of praise and condemnation. His use of violent imagery, such as the image of the "genius" breaking through the "hard crust" makes the reader feel like life in the city is violent and repressive. In contrast though, he repeats the superlative adjective "highest" in reference to the cities; this repetition emphasises his belief that cities can be a place where culture and civilisation reach their pinnacle. These opposing descriptions of the city combine overall to make cities seem hectic and stressful.

In contrast to the cities, Evans presents the countryside as having a calming influence over its inhabitants. He describes the "quiet and serious communion" that can be had with nature; the combination of gentle adjectives in this phrase shows the peacefulness of nature. Evans presents this peace as very positive because it allows "genius" to flourish, which contrasts with the "leveling" influence of the cities.

> This is good — it clearly evaluates the way that cities are presented in the text.

> This describes the way that the text makes the reader feel, which links it back to the question.

> Short, embedded quotes are used to support points without disturbing the flow of the answer.

1) This answer gives a clear evaluation of the text, backed up by relevant examples.

2) It could be improved by linking the second paragraph back to the effect on the reader.

This is a grade 8-9 answer extract

Lawton B. Evans presents a complex set of views on both cities and the country, which ultimately helps him to elucidate the importance of rural areas.

He makes it clear that there are impressive aspects of the city: for example, he describes cities as "centers of highest civilization"; this hyperbole indicates his admiration for the culture and art which flourishes in the city. However, he also describes the "leveling influence" of the city, which "merges individuals into masses". The alliterative 'm' sound in this phrase emphasises the amalgamating qualities of the city to the reader, leaving them with the impression that cities are somewhat restrictive and confining.

On the other hand, Evans portrays life in the countryside as "behind" in "development", which contrasts with the "civilization" of the cities. However, unlike the city, Evans believes that the countryside is set up to produce "The highest types of individuality". The adjective "ennobling", used to describe the effect of the countryside, links rural life to the lives of nobles and the aristocracy, and emphasises how influential Evans thinks the countryside can be in developing "great" individuals. These contrasts between the country and the city help Evans to persuade the reader that it is important to focus on rural areas, because they can have an important and influential effect on society.

> Talking about the writer's purpose is a good way to introduce how the text affects the reader.

> This describes clearly how the text makes the reader think and feel.

> This analyses a key word in detail, which helps to support the point being made.

This answer makes some interesting and original points. It gives a good overview of the text as well as making detailed points about the effect it has on the reader.

Graded Answers — Question A5

Question A5 is the first of two questions that ask you to write about both texts in your answer. Have another look at the question on page 77, then have a read through these answers.

Explain the writers' viewpoints on a particular topic

1) In your answer to question A5, you need to show that you can <u>pick out information</u> from <u>both</u> sources about a particular topic, then summarise it in your <u>own words</u>.

> A summary is a piece of writing that <u>combines</u> the ideas from both texts — have a look at p.13 if you need a reminder.

2) Even though you're writing in your own words, you should still include <u>evidence</u> from the texts to support the points you're making.

3) The question asks you to pick out information about <u>education</u> in <u>rural areas</u> — so you should only include points that focus on that topic, and not anything else.

4) There's no need to <u>compare</u> the two writers' opinions — you just need to <u>explain</u> them clearly and fully, in as <u>concise</u> a way as possible.

5) This question is only worth <u>four marks</u>, so don't waste time giving lots of <u>unnecessary detail</u>.

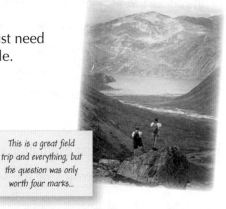

> *This is a great field trip and everything, but the question was only worth four marks...*

Here's a grade 4-5 answer extract

> Both writers think that rural education is important. Rishi Sunak thinks it needs to be focused on because lots of schools are currently "under-funded" and the problems are not "well understood". Lawton B. Evans, on the other hand, thinks that rural education needs improving because the countryside is underdeveloped: he says it is "behind" the city. Evans also says that cities attract everything "good and bad alike".

> *This does summarise something that both writers say, but to answer the question properly it needs to clearly summarise why both writers think this.*

> *This isn't necessary — you don't need to make comparisons between the two texts for this question.*

> *This is good — using short quotes as evidence from the text.*

> *This point doesn't answer the question.*

1) This makes some points about <u>both texts</u>, that are backed up by <u>relevant examples</u>.

2) It needs to stay <u>focused</u> on the question — some points <u>aren't relevant</u>.

3) It could also be improved by <u>combining</u> the writers' viewpoints so there's a clearer <u>overview</u> of the reasons why rural education needs to be focused on.

4) It should also avoid <u>comparing</u> the writers' viewpoints — this question just asks you to <u>summarise</u> what the writers are saying.

Graded Answers — Question A5

Here's a grade 6-7 answer extract

Both writers suggest that rural schools need to be focused on because if they are improved it will have a positive impact on their whole communities. Rishi Sunak says that they are the "beating hearts" of small villages and that education is the most important thing to "make an impact". Lawton B. Evans says that improved rural education would make the rural population "content", "enlightened" and "prosperous".

The writers also state that it's unfair that rural schools have been neglected in favour of the cities: Rishi Sunak gives examples of the funding differences between schools in different areas, and Lawton B. Evans says that development of urban schools has come "at the expense" of rural schools.

> This makes a clear point that summarises something that both texts are saying.

> You can paraphrase the text or quote it directly to support your points.

1) This clearly summarises some aspects of the writers' arguments, and some good examples are used from both texts to back up the points being made.

2) It could be improved by giving more of an overview of what both writers are saying.

Here's a grade 8-9 answer extract

The two writers give a variety of reasons to explain why education in rural areas needs to be more focused on. For example, they suggest that rural education needs to be focused on because the current situation is unfair. This is demonstrated by Sunak's description of the "raw deal" that many schools receive, and Evans's explanation that the development of city schools comes at the "expense" of rural schools.

The writers also argue that rural education needs to be focused on because of the positive effect it could have on the wider community. Sunak says that education allows people to "make an impact" in their community, and Evans explains that improved rural education would increase productivity in the "fields" and on the "farm", thereby making them more "prosperous". In addition, Evans implies that focusing more on rural education would mean that society produced more "great men", because rural people would have more time to devote to "culture and the higher arts".

It is therefore clear that rural education needs a greater focus because, if improved, it would have a positive impact on rural communities and society as a whole.

> This is a good opening — it shows that the answer is going to give an overview of the reasons given in both texts.

> This sentence summarises the writers' viewpoints without comparing them.

> This summarises the evidence in the paragraph in a concise way.

This is great — it gives a more comprehensive overview of the two writers' viewpoints, and it combines both writers' arguments in a clear and concise way.

Graded Answers — Question A6

Question A6 is worth another 10 marks. Take a look back at the question on page 77, then have a read through these answers. You might just pick up some tips that will save your life... well, help you out a bit.

Compare the writers' different points of view

1) Question A6 is about what the writers <u>think</u> about education, as well as <u>how they show</u> what they're thinking.

2) The question is asking you to <u>compare</u>, so you need to write about the <u>similarities</u> and <u>differences</u> between the writers' attitudes, and <u>link</u> them together using words and phrases such as 'however', 'in contrast' or 'whereas'.

3) There are some handy bullet points to guide you — you need to read them <u>carefully</u> and cover what they <u>ask for</u> in your answer.

> - You need to identify what the writers' <u>attitudes</u> to <u>education</u> are, and clearly <u>compare</u> them.
> - You also need to compare <u>how</u> the writers have shown their attitudes to education, i.e. the <u>words</u>, <u>phrases</u> and <u>language techniques</u> they've used.

Sam knew exactly how he felt about education.

4) You should focus on the writers' attitudes to <u>education</u>, not anything else.

5) You should back up every point you make with relevant <u>evidence</u> from the text — using <u>short quotations</u> is a great way to do this.

Here's a grade 4-5 answer extract

Rishi Sunak believes that rural schools should be given more money, whereas Lawton B. Evans believes that it is not money but attention that rural schools need. For example, Sunak says that schools should all receive their "fair share" of funding, but that currently many schools are "under-funded". He repeats the idea of "fair share", which shows how important he thinks it is.

In contrast, Lawton B. Evans is fixed on the idea that people's "thought" and "study" has been focused on schools in the city for too long, but he doesn't mention money. He thinks that people in rural areas could "live more comfortably and more happily", and that education can help them achieve this. This shows that he thinks it's important to pay more attention to education because it can improve the lives of people living in rural communities.

> This answer starts with a good comparison point.

> This is good — it picks up on a technique that the writer uses and comments on how it is used to convey the writer's point of view.

> This is a good point, but it needs more explanation of <u>how</u> the writer conveys their argument.

1) This answer starts to explore the writers' <u>attitudes</u> and begins to comment on how <u>language</u> and <u>structure</u> are used to <u>show</u> those attitudes.

2) However, it could go into more detail by using more <u>examples</u>, and explaining them more <u>clearly</u> and <u>accurately</u>.

Graded Answers — Question A6

Here's a grade 6-7 answer extract

Both writers say that education is an important part of society. In the newspaper article by Rishi Sunak, the text is structured so that the same idea is repeated at the beginning and end of the article: that education is the "greatest single tool" that can allow you to "change" your "life". By presenting this idea at the beginning and end of the article, Sunak emphasises how important he feels it is: he clearly wants the reader to remember what he is saying.

Lawton B. Evans also uses the structure of his article to convey the idea that education is an important part of society. For example, in the third paragraph he uses repetition, starting several sentences in a row with the phrase "We need". The use of the verb "need" in this phrase emphasises that a good-quality education is not just desirable, but necessary for all members of society. The concepts he introduces, such as "skilled" labour and "intelligent" farm management, show the reader that there are many positive effects of education, which encourages them to agree with Evans's idea that better education in rural areas will have a positive impact on local communities.

> 'Cyclical' would have been a better technical term to describe this structure.

> This answer clearly compares how the two writers get across their arguments.

> This answer consistently covers the bullet points — what the writers' attitudes are and how they're conveyed — and good quotes are used to back up each point.

This answer could be improved by comparing the writers' techniques in more detail...

This is a grade 8-9 answer extract

Both writers are attempting to persuade their respective readerships that there are flaws in the current educational system; to do this, they both use an assured tone that suggests the factual, reliable nature of the information they are presenting to the reader.

Rishi Sunak creates this tone using a variety of examples and statistics, which underline the injustice he perceives in the education system. For example, he describes how a pupil in "one of the top five funded areas" in the country receives "£2,000 more" than pupils in North Yorkshire. This statistic suggests that Sunak's stance is well-researched and grounded in reality, which helps to contribute to the overall confident tone in the article.

Lawton B. Evans, on the other hand, does not include statistical evidence; nevertheless, his choice of language means that his article has a similar tone to Rishi Sunak's. He explains that rural residents, when educated, "will accomplish as much as now in far less time", and "will live more comfortably and more happily". In phrases such as these, the verb "will" emphasises Evans's certainty about the effects of improving education in rural areas, creating a general tone of confidence that strengthens his argument and mirrors the tone of Sunak's article.

> This starts by clearly comparing the purpose of both texts, then goes on to write about the methods that the writers use.

> These phrases show that you're continuously comparing the two writers.

> This is a good, detailed analysis of how the writer's language conveys their argument.

This answer is really good — it makes a clear, sustained comparison of the writers' views, and it discusses in depth how each writer conveys their ideas.

Graded Answers — Question B1

Section B has two big writing questions in it. Here are some example answers for question B1 — take a look back at the question on page 77, then enjoy the feast of non-fiction writing before you...

Question B1 asks you to advise and inform the reader

1) For question B1, you need to give the reader some information and use it to advise them on what to do.

2) You need to match your writing to the form, purpose and audience you've been given in the question.

> • The form is a report — so you could use an impersonal, objective tone to convey your ideas to the reader.
>
> • The purpose is to inform and advise the reader, so you need to structure your answer in a logical way, with a clear introduction and conclusion.
>
> • The audience is your school governors. This means you need to write in a way that appeals to an unfamiliar, adult audience.

There's some advice on how to write a report on p.58.

3) Don't forget there are 8 marks on offer for spelling, punctuation and grammar for this question, so it's really important to write accurately and clearly, with a good range of vocabulary (see p.10-11).

Here's a grade 4-5 answer extract

> This report suggests that the school sets up several extra-curricular clubs, which will help to encourage students to take up outdoor hobbies. Examples could include traditional clubs such as tennis, football, hockey and netball, or unusual options such as bird-watching or mountain climbing. The unusual options will be less familiar to students, which might make them seem more exciting or appealing. Offering a range of different activities will be key to the success of this plan.
>
> To persuade students to take up these hobbies, it would be a good idea to advertise them through the school, including in the newsletter and in school assemblies. If teachers are enthusiastic enough and they make the benefits of outdoor activities clear, then students will surely be persuaded to take part. This will lead to a healthier, happier and more active school population.
>
> The school could also offer residential school trips, such as camping. These can be a nightmare to organise, but they are exciting for students and will encourage them to continue doing outdoor activities after the trip is over. They also provide an opportunity for students to make friends, which was an added bonus for the overall happiness and harmony of the school.

For a report, it would be better to start with a clear introductory paragraph instead of just one sentence.

This is a good range of ideas for activities that students might enjoy, and it responds clearly to one of the bullet points in the question.

This isn't relevant to the question.

This is a bit informal — it's not really appropriate for the audience or form.

This doesn't quite make sense — the wrong tense has been used. This would lose you marks for technical accuracy.

1) This answer clearly responds to the bullet points in the question by suggesting outdoor hobby ideas and exploring ways to persuade students.

2) However, the structure isn't very sophisticated, and the language could be more interesting and complex.

Graded Answers — Question B1

Here's a grade 6-7 answer extract

The following report outlines the best ways to encourage students to take up a wider variety of outdoor hobbies. This report contains suggestions for activities in which students might wish to participate, and also offers some suggestions regarding how the school might go about persuading reluctant students to take part.

Having closely considered the options, this report has concluded that most teenagers prefer to take part in activities that are more unusual or exciting than the norm. As such, activities such as rowing or hiking are likely to be more popular than commonplace activities such as athletics or ball games. It is useful to bear these preferences in mind when appealing to students to take up a new activity.

It can be difficult to persuade students to start doing outdoor activities. This report recommends making use of all the options available to the school; in particular, PE lessons could be used as a means of introducing students to a variety of enjoyable activities that they might wish to take up on a regular basis at a later date.

This answer responds to the bullet points in a way that's appropriate for the form.

A confident, assured tone is appropriate when writing to inform and advise.

This answer is clearly structured using paragraphs, but they could be more fluently linked together.

1) This answer is well suited to the form, purpose and audience given in the question, and it covers the bullet points clearly.

2) It could be improved by having a more imaginative structure and by using more interesting language.

Here's a grade 8-9 answer extract

This opening sentence makes it clear what the report will be about.

This report explores possible ways that Dynor Secondary School could encourage greater participation in outdoor hobbies, as raised by the school governors at a PTA meeting on Wednesday 7th December. At the meeting it was concluded that the school would like to play a more active role in encouraging outdoor hobbies; this report explores possibilities in this regard, as well as offering suggestions for accessible outdoor hobbies that students might enjoy.

Access is perhaps the greatest barrier for students at Dynor Secondary School; as an urban school, hobbies such as hiking or climbing are often impractical. It is therefore suggested that the school focus its energies on promoting outdoor activities that are appropriate for an urban environment. From research conducted within the local community, it has been determined that these are likely to consist of group sports activities, such as football, basketball and hockey. Given the sociable nature of most outdoor sports games, it is hoped that students will require minimal persuasion to take part; nevertheless, the remainder of this report will present some ideas for increased participation, making full use of the channels of promotion available within Dynor Secondary School.

This is a nice, subtle way to link two paragraphs together.

Formal language like this is appropriate for an informative report.

Complex sentence structures like this will impress the examiner.

This is a great answer — it's appropriate for the form, purpose and audience, and it uses complex, interesting language and sentence structures.

Section Six — Paper 2: Sample Exam and Graded Answers

Graded Answers — Question B2

To B2, or not to B2? The answer's pretty obvious — you really do need to answer both writing questions for paper 2. Look back at the question on page 77, then take a look at these nifty sample answers.

Adapt your writing style to the question

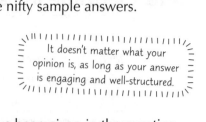
It doesn't matter what your opinion is, as long as your answer is engaging and well-structured.

1) For B2, you need to give your <u>own perspective</u> on the council's idea to encourage people under the age of 16 to have part-time jobs.

2) You need to match your writing to the <u>form</u>, <u>purpose</u> and <u>audience</u> you've been given in the question.

> • The <u>form</u> is a broadsheet newspaper article — so you could write in the style of an <u>opinion piece</u> with lots of <u>personality</u> (see pages 53-55 for more on this).
>
> • The <u>purpose</u> is to <u>explain</u> your point of view, which you could do by making an <u>argument</u> for your viewpoint.
>
> • The <u>audience</u> isn't mentioned specifically, but you can <u>work it out</u>. It's a broadsheet newspaper article about working under the age of 16, so it's likely to be read by <u>adults</u> who have <u>children</u> of around that age.

3) It's also important to think about the <u>structure</u> of your writing, especially the <u>opening</u> and <u>ending</u>. You need to <u>link</u> your paragraphs together clearly, too.

4) Don't forget there are 8 marks on offer for <u>spelling</u>, <u>punctuation</u> and <u>grammar</u> for this question — it's really important to write <u>accurately</u> and <u>clearly</u> with a good range of <u>vocabulary</u> (see p.10-11).

Here's a grade 4-5 answer extract

This opening sentence isn't really appropriate for a broadsheet newspaper.

This answer uses a counter-argument to strengthen the point it's making.

A new paragraph should start here.

The repetition of rhetorical questions is a nice language feature here — it makes the point of view come across more forcefully.

<u>NO PART-TIME JOBS FOR UNDER-SIXTEENS</u>

I think that children under the age of 16 shouldn't get a part-time job. Although some people might argue that having a job teaches children about the value of money, time management and working as a team, I don't think that this is the case.

Firstly, most children already have good time management skills. Schools start at 9 am, and some even earlier than this, so arriving on time to lessons is already second nature to most children. Why should children have a part-time job when they already know how to manage their time? Secondly, most children have been working as a team since primary school. From sports teams in P.E., to group projects in Science, school teaches children how to work together from a very young age. Why should children give up their weekends for a badly paid job when they already have great teamwork skills?

1) This answer makes some <u>good points</u> that are focused on the <u>question</u>.

2) It could be better matched to the <u>form</u> that the question asks for, though — the <u>tone</u> and <u>style</u> aren't always appropriate for a <u>broadsheet newspaper</u>.

3) The language could also be more varied and interesting — including a bit of <u>humour</u> or using more <u>creative vocabulary</u> would gain more marks.

Bradley's part-time job taught him to dress for success.

Section Six — Paper 2: Sample Exam and Graded Answers

Graded Answers — Question B2

Here's a grade 6-7 answer extract

SAVE THE LEARNING FOR THE CLASSROOM

Lots of young people have a part-time job, and I am sure that employment teaches them a whole host of valuable skills: communication, time management and independence to name but a few. However, these skills aren't just learnt in the workplace; many young people develop and refine these skills in the classroom.

Take, for instance, communication. Every day in school, pupils communicate with a wide range of people. Pupils learn to talk respectfully to teachers; they learn how to make engaging conversation with their friends; and they learn how to communicate their ideas effectively to their peers during group work. School doesn't just allow pupils to practise their verbal communication — it allows them to develop their written communication too. Essays teach students how to summarise their thoughts, and present their opinions. What part-time job could develop communication more effectively than this?

The answer uses sophisticated punctuation accurately.

The tone of this answer is suitable for the form and purpose. It's a bit more chatty than the previous answer, but it still uses good vocabulary.

The ideas are linked together fluently.

1) This answer uses language techniques, a clear structure and creative vocabulary to get its point across.

2) However, if the author's personality came across more strongly, the text would be more compelling.

Here's a grade 8-9 answer extract

MINIMUM WAGE, MINIMUM GAIN

Part-time jobs have little value for teenagers under sixteen, argues Charlie Lin.

If someone were to ask me whether I thought under-sixteens should get part-time jobs, my answer, unequivocally, would be "no". As I write this, I can imagine the shocked looks on my readers' faces and the disdainful cries of "but employment teaches children valuable life skills!" To these critics, I say this: there's nothing a part-time job can teach children that they can't learn from other, more rewarding options.

If you don't believe me, then think about the jobs that are actually available to under-sixteens. Paper rounds, waiting tables, shop assistant — essentially an assortment of mundane, badly-paid Saturday jobs. And what 'valuable life skills' might they learn while toiling away for less than minimum wage? "Teamwork!" you might cry triumphantly, "working in a cafe would teach a young person how to work as part of a team." This may certainly be true if you believe being belittled by the chef and bossed around by the manager counts as 'teamwork'. I, however, do not. If that same child was part of a football team, working alongside their peers, practising hard to achieve a common goal (annihilating the rival team), now that would be teamwork.

A headline and strapline are used to grab the reader's attention.

The writer shows a clear awareness of their audience.

Really interesting and varied vocabulary makes this answer high-level.

Lots of rhetorical techniques are used in this paragraph to make the writer's point of view clear and their argument compelling.

A sarcastic tone makes the argument convincingly, but also gives a sense of the writer's personality.

The writer's opinion and personality is clear in this answer, and it's fluently written. The tone is humorous and chatty, but also subtle, which makes the answer engaging and readable.

Glossary

alliteration	When words that are <u>close together</u> start with the <u>same sound</u>. E.g. "the <u>b</u>eat of the <u>b</u>and".
analogy	A <u>comparison</u> to show how one thing is <u>similar</u> to another, which makes it easier to <u>understand</u> or more <u>memorable</u>. E.g. "watching cricket is about as exciting as watching paint dry."
antithesis	A technique where <u>opposing</u> words or ideas are presented <u>together</u> to show a contrast.
audience	The <u>person</u> or <u>group of people</u> that read or listen to a text.
biased writing	Gives <u>more support</u> to one point of view than to another because of the writer's <u>own opinions</u>.
broadsheet	A more <u>formal</u> type of newspaper, which often focuses on more <u>serious</u> topics. E.g. *The Guardian* or *The Telegraph*.
clause	Part of a sentence that has a <u>subject</u> and a <u>verb</u>. <u>Main clauses</u> make sense on their own.
colloquial language	<u>Informal</u> language that sounds like ordinary <u>speech</u>.
commentary (newspaper article)	A type of newspaper article that expresses the <u>opinions</u> of the writer on a theme or news event. Also called a <u>column</u>, <u>opinion piece</u>, or <u>editorial</u>.
connotations	The <u>suggestions</u> that words can make <u>beyond</u> their obvious meaning.
counter-argument	The <u>opposite</u> point of view to the writer's own view. This is useful when writing to argue or persuade — first give the counter-argument, then explain why you <u>disagree</u> with it.
direct address	When a writer talks <u>straight to the reader</u>, e.g. "you might recall..."
emotive language	Language that has an <u>emotional</u> effect on the reader.
explicit information	Information that's <u>directly stated</u> in a text.
figurative language	Language that is used in a <u>non-literal</u> way to create an effect, e.g. personification.
first person	A <u>narrative viewpoint</u> where the narrator is one of the <u>characters</u>.
flashback	A writing technique where the scene shifts from the <u>present</u> to an event in the <u>past</u>.
form	The <u>type</u> of text, e.g. a letter, a speech or a newspaper article.
hyperbole	When <u>exaggeration</u> is used to have an <u>effect</u> on the reader.
imagery	A type of <u>figurative language</u> that creates a <u>picture in your mind</u>, e.g. metaphors and similes.
impersonal tone	A tone of writing that <u>doesn't</u> try to directly <u>engage</u> with the reader.
implicit information	Information that's hinted at <u>without</u> being said outright.
inference	A <u>conclusion</u> reached about something, based on <u>evidence</u>. E.g. from the sentence "Yasmin wrinkled her nose at the lasagne", you could <u>infer</u> that Yasmin doesn't like lasagne.
inversion	Altering the <u>normal word order</u> for <u>emphasis</u>, e.g. "On the table sat a hedgehog."
irony	Saying one thing but <u>meaning the opposite</u>.
limited narrator	A narrator who only has <u>partial knowledge</u> about the events or characters in a story.
linear structure	A type of narrative structure that tells the events of a story in <u>chronological</u> order.
list of three	Using <u>three</u> words (often adjectives) or phrases together to create <u>emphasis</u>.

Glossary

metaphor	A way of describing something by saying that it is something else, to create a vivid image. E.g. "His eyes were deep blue pools."
motif	A recurring image or idea in a text.
narrative	Writing that tells a story or describes an experience.
narrative viewpoint	The perspective that a text is written from, e.g. first-person point of view.
non-linear structure	A type of narrative structure that tells the events of a story in a non-chronological order.
objective writing	A neutral, unbiased style of writing which contains facts rather than opinions.
omniscient narrator	A narrator who knows the thoughts and feelings of all the characters in a narrative.
onomatopoeia	A word that imitates the sound it describes as you say it, e.g. 'whisper'.
pace	The speed at which the writer takes the reader through the events in a story.
paraphrase	Describing or rephrasing something in a text without including a direct quote.
parenthesis	A rhetorical technique where an extra clause or phrase is inserted into a complete sentence.
personification	Describing a non-living thing as if it's a person. E.g. "The sea growled hungrily."
purpose	The reason someone writes a text. E.g. to persuade, to argue, to advise, to inform.
register	The specific language used to match writing to the social situation that it's for.
repetition	The technique of repeating words for effect.
rhetoric	Using language techniques (e.g. repetition or hyperbole) to achieve a persuasive effect.
rhetorical question	A question that doesn't need an answer. E.g. "Why do we do this to ourselves?"
sarcasm	Language that has a scornful or mocking tone, often using irony.
satire	A style of text that makes fun of something, often by imitating it and exaggerating its flaws.
second person	A narrative viewpoint that is written as if the reader is one of the characters.
sensory language	Language that appeals to the five senses.
simile	A way of describing something by comparing it to something else, usually by using the words 'like' or 'as'. E.g. "He was as pale as the moon."
slang	Words or phrases that are informal, and often specific to one age group or social group.
Standard English	English that is considered correct because it uses formal features of spelling and grammar.
structure	The order and arrangement of ideas in a text. E.g. how the text begins, develops and ends.
style	The way in which a text is written, e.g. the type of language, sentence forms and structure used.
tabloid	A less formal type of newspaper, which often focuses on more sensational topics.
third person	A narrative viewpoint where the narrator remains outside the events of the story.
tone	The mood or feeling of a piece of writing, e.g. happy, sad, serious, light-hearted.
viewpoint	The attitude and beliefs that a writer is trying to convey.

Index

19th-century texts
  examples 13, 20, 24, 36, 79
  reading and understanding
    23, 24

A

adjectives 27, 28
adverbs 27, 28
alliteration 32, 35, 44, 60
analogy 30
antithesis 35
articles (text type) 53-55
assessment objectives 2
audience
  for reading 14
  for writing 48, 49

B

bias 9, 16, 22, 36, 40
broadsheets 54

C

clauses 35, 42
commands 42
commentaries (articles) 53
complex sentences 14, 42
compound sentences 42
correcting mistakes 11
creative writing 50-52
cumulative effects 28

D

descriptive language 37
determiners 27
direct address 50

E

essays 58
exam structure 1
exclamations 42, 60
explaining words and phrases 6, 9
explicit information 2, 12

F

finding information
    12, 16, 65, 80, 83

G

grammar 10, 11

H

headlines 44, 45, 54
hyperbole 35, 36

I

imagery 29-31, 37, 75
implicit information 2, 8, 9, 12
irony 33, 34

L

language
  colloquial 26, 48, 53
  emotive 18, 20
leaflets 56
letters 61
linking words and phrases 7
list of three 35, 60
literature 21
literary non-fiction 22

M

metaphors 29, 37

N

narrative viewpoint 38, 40, 51
narrator 21, 38
nouns 27

O

onomatopoeia 32

P

paragraphs 7
paraphrasing 5
parenthesis 35
P.E.E.D. 4-7
personification 31, 37
planning 3, 46
presentation 44, 45
pronouns 19, 27, 46
punctuation 10, 11, 25

purpose
  for reading 15-19
  for writing 46, 47

Q

questions (sentence type) 42
quotes 5

R

register 26, 46, 48, 53
repetition 21, 28
reports 58
reviews 59
rhetoric 18, 35, 53
rhetorical questions 35, 46, 60

S

sarcasm 34, 53
semantic field 28
sentence forms 42, 43
similes 29, 37
simple sentences 42
speeches 60
spelling 10, 11
Standard English 6
statements 42
structure 39-41
style 26, 46, 48
subheadings 44, 54
summarising information
    13, 86, 87

T

tabloids 54
tone 20, 25, 46, 48, 53
travel writing 57

V

verbs 27

W

words and phrases
    27, 28, 51, 66, 68
word types 27
writer's attitudes 8, 20, 86-89

FNWR41